Planning and Planting a Garden

New Illustrated Library of Home Improvement Volume 8

Planning and Planting a Garden

Prentice-Hall/Reston Editorial Staff

Prentice-Hall of Canada, Ltd. / Reston Publishing Company

Scarborough, Ontario

*Series contributors/*H. Fred Dale, Richard Demske, George R.
Drake, Byron W. Maguire, L. Donald Meyers, Gershon
Wheeler

*Design/*Peter Maher & Associates

Printed and bound in Canada

The publishers wish to thank the following
for providing photographs for this volume:
American Association of Nurserymen
Better Lawn and Turf Institute
Canadian Association of Nurserymen
Canadian Department of Agriculture
H. Fred Dale
Ferry Morse Seed Co.
Malak
National Garden Bureau
The Netherlands Flower-bulb Institute
Sheridan Nurseries
Yoder Brothers
The drawings on pages 21, 22, 26, 30 and 31 are by James Loates.

Contents

Preface

This volume is intended to assist the reader to plan the best use of the soil and available space for lawn and garden. The combination of trees, shrubs and flowers for the most pleasing effect is considered, bearing in mind soil and climate conditions. Specific planting techniques are treated in Volume 13 of this series.

The planting seasons and viability of the plants included are generally those of the central North American region, with specific variations noted (e.g., Pacific coast, prairies). You should check with your local nurseryman and agricultural experimental station for further details on specific plants and their growing seasons if you live in a subtropical, subarctic or desert climate.

Gardening: Arranging Nature to Suit Us

If agriculture is growing plants for food commercially, horticulture is the science of growing decorative plants, and landscape architecture is the profession of arranging land, rock and plants into a pleasing or dramatic pattern, what then is gardening? In part it's a little bit of each of the others. It's also something more and something less.

Although you can save money by growing your own vegetables, cutting your own grass and doing your own pruning, gardening is not a commercial enterprise, for once you start providing services for others for a fee you pass into another category — landscape contractor, garden maintenance, market-gardener, greenhouseman or nurseryman.

Gardening has a natural quality about it. You are working with basic, real, whole, live things where there is no memo writing and no office politics. When you create a picture in your garden or on your window sill, you're in it from start to finish. In that way it has something in common with art, writing or music. That is one reason why it is so soothing to those of us whose lives are fragmented, or whose daily job offers few satisfactions beyond the money every week.

In a sense, gardening is taming nature. In this sense gardening is keeping in touch with the natural growing cycle, with the four seasons which thus mark off the segments of the year. To the gardener a killing frost is an event as real as a traffic accident witnessed. It

may be a disaster or it may simply mark the end of the growing season for another year. But the gardener feels it as far more of an event than someone who merely notes that an extra sweater seems in order.

A summer drought brings anguish — and a lot of extra work watering — to the gardener while another person might simply feel that sunny weather is his due as a swimmer or sunbather. The relief a gardener feels when that drought is broken by a heavy rainstorm is so great it can be tasted — have you ever walked in a downpour in the garden to watch the water being absorbed in the dry soil, and to see plants becoming turgid and greener by the moment? We've suffered as wet snow or ice storms bent and broke evergreens, and fumed and worked furiously to rid plants of an insect infestation. Or we've died a little too in watching seedling trees fail to survive their first summer, or perhaps just barely tolerated the destruction of other trees and vegetable garden plants by groundhogs and neighboring children.

The one thing gardening won't permit is indifference. Nor, however, can a gardener be content to simply let nature take its course. Most gardeners appreciate wilderness areas, natural forests, unspoiled river courses. But these untamed, wild places are not gardens. Gardening is connected and involved with nature and natural things, but it also consists in controlling nature as best we can. A lawn is a perfect example. No wild grassy meadow, nor farmer's meadow, consists only of grasses of certain kinds with no unwanted plants (weeds). Nor do the natural meadows, like lawns, have grass plants growing so close together you can't see the soil when they are kept cut to three inches or lower.

A beautifully formed, lone tree rarely occurs naturally. Strawberries in the wild compete with each other, with grass and with other plants for space, light and water. As a result the berries are few and tiny. Some other plants we commonly accept as part of gardening would soon die out if left to their own devices. Grafted, hybrid roses are a good example. In fact few plants we grow in our gardens are natives from the wild. Most have been bred or selected for their garden values, not their ability to survive on their own. Not only that, we know that plants, like people, grow better and perform better with superior nutrition and enough room to develop their potential.

Gardening is thus the business of creating the best environment possible so that our plants will be superior to what they would be if left alone. We try to get the perfect rose bloom, the more prolific garden pea plant, the unwormy apple, the hedge with thick foliage to the ground, the picture postcard evergreen. Or it may be the reverse — getting a plant to grow in an unnatural environment. Gardeners in cold climates do this with roses and with plants normally considered too tender. Consider the house plant in a modern apartment which gets virtually cave light in the dark months of the year, and suffers from air with less humidity than that of the Sahara Desert. Our aim is to keep it green and lush-looking. Or we may try to maintain a forest size tree in a container, or attempt to grow peaches or grapes far north of their natural limit.

In all these ways gardening consists in trying to arrange nature to suit us. Fortunately we don't have to start from the very beginning and learn every step on our own.

Gardening has a long history. It's said that man first settled down to till the land, not to assure a regular supply of grain for flour for bread, but to guarantee barley for beer. The next step was to select a better strain of barley.

Along the way we've picked up a good deal of knowledge on how plants operate and how we can help them to do it better — their needs for water, minerals, kinds of soil, day length, cold dormancy and heat dormancy, and their susceptibility to insect and disease infestations. Applying this information is the science of gardening. Learn to see things from the plants' point of view. Give them what they need — not what you'd like them to have — and they'll respond with better growth.

But gardening is also an art, regarded in Europe as one of the highest kinds of art; without a knowledge of it no one is considered truly educated. The art of gardening is what you bring to it: your eye, your creativeness, your arrangement of the picture you make around your house, on your balcony, in your living room, on your window sill.

If, as is commonly said, your patio (or balcony) is an extension of your living room, the whole garden is an extension of your personality.

Gardening consists in avoiding cliché plantings, in choosing kinds and varieties of plants that get along well together, and that allow you to engage in many kinds of activities in comfort among them. It consists in choosing plants with some garden interest in all of the four seasons, in having room for special favorites. But it also consists in suiting the plantings to the kind of maintenance you can afford to give them. No one who is not prepared for careful and sometimes tedious weeding, watering and dividing, for example, should plant a rock garden just because they like the idea of a rock garden — in lush color photos such gardens appear self-maintaining. Nor by the same token should you plant a vegetable, flower, rose or any other special garden within the property that is larger than you can comfortably look after. Or, as the old joke has it, don't plant a vegetable garden larger than your wife or husband can look after.

In this first volume of two on gardening in this series on home improvement, we'll deal with some of the basic, simple ideas you can use to help make gardening easier and to make your garden both look better and suit your needs. There is nothing necessarily complicated about planning a garden any more than there is in planting it, if you bear in mind some of the principles and techniques available. But as well as from the ideas in this volume, home gardeners can learn from private gardens they visit, from garden lay-outs at flower shows, and from trial and error experiments of their own. Public parks and demonstration gardens may offer ideas that are also adaptable to home gardens, but remember in such cases to scale everything down to the size of the property you are working with.

In Volume 13 of this series actual planting techniques will be covered, with step by step instructions, and with specific plants for different purposes and their care. The aim is to make gardening more enjoyable because that's the name of the game. Whenever you get too worried or too serious about a garden problem, stop and tell yourself to remember the reason for gardening in the first place: to make life more pleasant.

2 What Do You Want from that Ground around Your House?

An English immigrant once said that he couldn't stand the North American word "yard" to describe the front and back garden because it sounded so much like a commercial area or one associated with a jail. Yet in practice it may be very appropriate. So many of our front and back areas are merely yards; they are not gardens. What garden there is just grew, with no direction and very little help from the occupant of the house.

Even in many cases where the gardener does show an interest in growing things, the garden is merely a collection of plants, often unrelated in their shape, size, texture and leaf or flower colors; similarly, many indoor gardeners have a collection of plants, but not an indoor garden.

2-1. Arranging the Yard

Backyards of expensive suburban and city houses often have a jumble of clothesline, tricycles, sandbox, swing set, patio stones and plants that seem to interfere with free movement between. And who hasn't seen and exclaimed on the ugliness of an above-the-ground swimming pool stuck in the dead center of a tiny yard? In cold climates that yard is useless for all but a few weeks when the weather is hot enough to warrant jumping in the pool.

No one living in a house is under the delusion there won't be garbage and thus the need for a place to store it between pickups. People with children know there will be toy trucks, tricycles (and later bicycles), probably sandboxes and swing sets. You can't comfortably sit outside when the grass is wet if you don't have a paved area; that paved area will be used mostly by the adults in the family. So it makes sense to separate it from the play and service areas.

There will be at least some garden equipment — a mower, perhaps gasoline storage cans, a rake or two, a scuffle hoe, weeding tool, fertilizer and peat moss supply.

And finally there will be the actual garden areas: the lawn, the shrubs, bulb plantings, annual flowers, a vegetable garden (if only for salad greens and tomatoes) and room for the specialty garden such as roses, herbs, dahlias, or whatever the gardener's particular interest.

All of these requirements, plus easy access to the house, driveway and street, must be accommodated in one way or another. The way you arrange the whole will determine whether you have a yard or garden. A yard will contain all these elements, but in no particular order and with no separation of the activities. A garden will separate the activities and screen one from another so that, for example, when sitting out on the patio after dinner with friends, you are not gazing on an unbroken vista of this week's laundry, the garbage cans, discarded bicycles, and stumbling over abandoned toys when you go to get a refill. Nor should the patio be located so far from the house door that the coffee is cold by the time you rejoin your friends. If your after-dinner gathering is in midsummer, it won't keep you cool to have the shade tree at the other end of the property from the sitting area, where it may shade the rose garden or a neighbor, but not you.

2-2. Landscaping

To everyone who asks how to landscape his or her property, we ask in turn: What do you want from it? What do you want it to look like? How much maintenance are you prepared to give it? Do you want to be able to play lawn games? For badminton there must be room for posts and a net, and for the players to move about. The turf must be tough enough to stand lots of foot traffic. This may take up all of a small lot whereas a horseshoe pit might nestle unobtrusively at the back end.

Do you want to eat meals outdoors without balancing plates and cups on your lap? Then you'll need to incorporate a picnic table in your garden plans. Room will have to be made for it where there is shade from a building or tree at the hottest time of the day you will use it. Perhaps a shade tree should be planted or, alternatively, a table umbrella or patio roof installed with material such as glass fiber that will filter the sun but let light through. This has the advantage of letting you cook and eat out even in the rain.

If you want a swimming pool you'll have to be prepared for it to dominate all but the largest properties. But there is no reason to settle for a rectangle of concrete placed dead center in the yard with tiny strips on each side that are very difficult to plant attractively, and which make no allowance for shade. You get no vista, and either you broil in the sun or stay in the water. Instead consider an oval, almond-shaped, kidney-shaped or other shape of pool that can add grace to the yard and will allow for plantings along the narrow end. Annual flowers in containers can provide

summer brightness at the pool's edge.

A deep-rooted tree such as an oak would not endanger the pool. Combined with some dwarf evergreens, it would bring a woodsy effect to the edge of the pool and if pool and planting were arranged according to the exposure to the sun, could provide some welcome shade for anyone in danger of burning. It would also make a much more attractive picture from house windows in seasons when it was not comfortable to swim.

2-3. Using Plants for Screens

Do you need to shut off a view of the street or of neighbors? Then you'll have to arrange the plantings for screen purposes, perhaps at the expense of other things you might want to grow. Roses, vegetables and most annual flowers, for example, need a minimum of six hours' direct sunlight a day and do better in full sun. They won't do well and may fail if they have root competition from shrubs and trees. Obviously, serving one purpose may severely limit another.

Do you want a vista or the appearance of a closed garden from a house window or sliding glass doors? Then you'll want to arrange the yard space and choose your plants and their locations to promote that view even if it means sacrificing something else. Of course your property may be big enough to take into account all the uses you can think of.

Sometimes you may have to compromise to accommodate differing interests of the members of the household. Sunbathing and sitting in the shade may seem unreconcilable. But you might arrange your planting so there is sun till noon on a patch of grass, with shade during the heat of the afternoon for the sitter. On a large property, a sunning area could be screened for privacy by medium-height hedge plants in the sunniest part of the garden.

Sometimes a simple division will work. We know a woman who always slipped a tomato plant or two into her mother's bed of marigolds because the mother didn't like tomato plants. No one was happy until they agreed to divide up the area, using a low boxwood hedge as a division point. Now the mother doesn't discover tomatoes among her flowers and the daughter's tomatoes grow properly with the room they need. Once they agreed on what they wanted from the garden and decided to share it, the problem ended.

In another case, he wanted to grow showy dahlias and roses while she wanted vegetables for the table. The property was small, and simple division was not practical. By stating frankly what each expected from the grounds and by being prepared to compromise, they were both satisfied: he grew fewer showy flowers, she grew salad greens and tomatoes between them.

2-4. Use Low Hedges

One of the simplest ways to separate family activities and services is by low hedging, preferably with a hardy evergreen that requires virtually no maintenance. The plants may not actually be high enough to shut out the view entirely. They don't need to be and you might feel claustrophobic if they were. But even dwarf Arctic willow or Korean boxwood which seldom grow over two feet tall — at least not for years and years — make a psychological separation. And our experience is that if there is free access to each section of the garden, children don't go through the hedge.

For the service and shed or garden tool area, you might choose something that grows taller, say Japanese or hybrid yew (where hardy), or arborvitae (Eastern white cedar) in colder areas. These evergreens require only one basic pruning a year (with touch-up prunings at other times) and watering during droughts. For that minimum care, they provide year-round screening.

Nor do you need a great many divisions in a small garden. Sometimes from three to six plants will do the trick. You don't necessarily have to hide the service area entirely, but merely give the illusion of separation. Nor do

you necessarily need to have a gate across the entrance to the various areas. Two clipped evergreens with a passage between make a natural doorway that people like to pass through.

In a similar way you can mark off the rose or other garden with a low-growing plant arranged as a kind of hedge. This doesn't even have to be a perennial plant, shrub or evergreen. The purple-leafed basil (Dark Opal) can be used as a hedge to mark off a vegetable garden. It is not only decorative but edible.

To define the patio without actually enclosing it, for example, you might arrange a curved planting projecting from the property line. This could be filled with a mixture of low-growing plants, say a dwarf rose, a ball-shaped blue spruce with spring bulbs and a day lily or two. Of course on large properties, the patio could be entirely enclosed with hedging or attractive board fencing if the scale was large enough to give a feeling of space within. In this way you can create an outdoor living room, if that is what you want from the garden. This is just another example of defining the areas and while literally cutting down on the open space it may actually add to a feeling of room for each activity so defined.

2-5. How Much Maintenance?

When deciding on the kind of garden you want, it's unrealistic not to consider the kind of maintenance you are prepared to give it. Probably the easiest garden to maintain is the tiny fenced city lot paved with patio stones; where plants are grown in containers sitting on the patio and in pots or baskets hanging from the fence. This garden has a charm of its own but would not satisfy most home owners.

Next easiest to maintain is a yard with grass and one tree plus a flowering shrub or two. Mowing, clipping, weeding and fertilizing would not average more than half an hour a week. If the area is large enough and the grounds rolling, this simple treatment at best would be a natural-looking meadow with some shade for a lawn chair. At its worst it would be a level rectangle of grass, cooler-looking than pavement but essentially without interest. If you were to take that same uninteresting rectangular plot of grass, make some scallops of cultivated soil at the edges on the long dimensions, arrange a mixture of, say, spring-flowering shrubs, bulbs, a few evergreens for all-season interest and a place for some annual flowers, the dull rectangle would then become a garden. Maintenance would be greater, but mainly at the beginning when you plant the shrubs and bulbs. Thereafter, occasional weeding and spring planting of annual flowers would be the only additional work apart from looking after the grass.

It is obvious that for a slight additional increase in the work required to keep up such a garden, the dividends are very much greater. Now you can project this theory on to more complicated gardens. Take a rose garden, for example. It's going to take a lot more care than a similar-sized area sown to grass. What you have to do is ask yourself if it is worth the extra effort to you. No rose lover would hesitate, but there's a big difference between liking cut roses in a vase on the table, and being prepared to do the pruning, spraying, fertilizing, watering and providing winter protection that growing them well requires.

Similarly, everyone likes the idea of being able to pick vegetables in the garden within minutes of cooking them, knowing exactly what chemicals (if any) have been used on them. But the preparation, cultivation and care over the summer may be more than you are ready to give.

The most deceptive garden of all is the rock or alpine garden that always looks so good in color photos. The maintenance required is almost constant, what with weeding, watering, replacement of plants and soil and division of those that multiply freely.

Be realistic in your expectations. By all means plan a garden that suits your needs. But bear in mind what kind of garden you can realistically look after. It's far better for you to

start with a vegetable (or rose or bulb or perennial) garden that turns out to be too small to satisfy your needs, than to start out with one that is too large so you wind up neglecting it, which may turn you right off gardening. The former will likely whet your appetite for more, and you can increase the size a little each year until your needs and your time and energy are in balance.

In a similar way, the quality of your lawn will depend on the maintenance you can give it. It is unrealistic to expect lush, deep green, weed-free and vigorous grass if you don't fertilize, water, aerate and weed the lawn often enough, if you wear it thin and compact the soil with heavy foot traffic, or if you try to grow it over surface-rooting trees, such as poplars, maples, elms or willows.

Nor can you grow a first-quality lawn on the north side of a building where high-rise structures all round provide full, day-long, deep shade. Grass won't grow well on pure sands, heavy, unamended clays, or over large stones or rubble buried just under the soil surface, either.

2-6. Changing An Established Garden

No one likes the raw look of new subdivision houses where the only plants in sight are new sod and sapling trees. But they have the advantage of allowing you scope to plan and plant the kind of garden you want.

When you move into a house with an established garden it is not easy to get what you want from it immediately. The first thing to do is to make a survey of what is growing and how the garden is arranged.

Don't be in a hurry to make changes — it is probably worth waiting through one full growing season during which you can catalogue what is growing and where. There is no way in summer, for example, that you can know where spring-flowering bulbs are. Vines like clematis may have been cut down in fall and won't show their true colors until the next

June or July. Unless you recognize them by leaf or twig, you won't know if you like the flowering shrubs. It takes winter's bareness to enable one to see the outline of the planting.

After you have a clear idea of how the garden was planted (or at least of what is growing in it) you can start to make changes. Evergreen shrubs may be overgrown, creating a tangle rather than an attractive picture. The arrangement of the patio in the yard may not be convenient to the door. Perhaps one tree too many shades the area where you want a vegetable garden and its roots permeate the ground. In such cases it pays to be brutal; remove the offending plants and change the patio location.

Old hedges may have to be cut almost in half, not only to let you see out, but also to help them fill out thin areas near the ground. Remove entirely unsuitable hedge material such as Chinese or Siberian elms which quickly revert to trees without monthly shearings.

Clean out and relocate old perennial plantings. If these beds are overrun with weeds or weed grasses or both, spraying or repeated cultivation may be necessary before replanting.

Overgrown lilacs, climbing roses, forsythias and other shrubs can be thinned and renewed by removing all the older canes at ground level or where they originate. If they conflict with the way you want to use the land, remove them entirely at ground level, and run the power mower over the sprouts regularly until they stop coming up.

You can either remove plants or enlarge the cultivated areas allotted to them. As gardens mature, plants take up more and more room; unlike people, they continue to grow until they die. The only way to keep a balance between lawn and shrub or evergreen area is to rob the lawn to give to the shrubs.

If flower beds are too extensive for you to look after, grass them over. If shade is too extensive, remove all lower branches up to 20 or 30 feet or even higher so that filtered sunlight gets in. Remove any trees that are diseased, that threaten sewers or other utilities, or that prevent gardening under them.

2-7. Bringing A Thin Lawn Back

Revitalize old lawns on this basis: If more than 50 per cent of the lawn area is covered with grass, renovate. If less, till the old sod under, along with fertilizer and peat moss, and start again with seed or sod. Start renovations by aerating. This consists in running a spring-loaded aerator machine over the lawn area when the soil is damp after a heavy rain or watering, and is best done in spring as the frost comes out. The machine removes plugs of soil which opens up the ground to allow air, water and fertilizer to enter.

Next, apply a high-nitrogen lawn fertilizer (such as a 20:10:5, 10:6:4 or 12:4:8, the latter especially in sands) at recommended rates evenly over the whole lawn area. (See Sections 3-8 and 3-10 for explanation of the ratios.) Next comes an application of weedkiller. Use a combination product that will kill most narrow-leafed as well as broad-leafed weeds. If the fertilizer is broadcast and watered in several days before you apply the weedkiller, it will help make the herbicide more effective. Allow about 10 days for full effect. Then repeat the herbicide application if there are stubborn, old perennial weeds that didn't die.

Maintain a regular schedule of fertilizing and watering. Good perennial lawn grasses will likely fill in thin areas and bare spots vacated by the now-dead weeds. If this doesn't happen soon enough, you can sow fresh lawn grass seed lightly over the areas after scarifying (scratching the surface) to open the soil. This is a good time to introduce some of the newer, more vigorous blue-grasses and fescues. But remember that the best time to sow grass is in early spring as soon as you can work the land, or for a month at the end of August.

The Soil Is the Key

We dig it, we move it, we plant it, we fertilize it, we write about it and we curse it. But most of us don't really know what our garden soil is or how it works. Soil began with disintegration of rock, a process which continues today. The erosion of wind and water, the cracking action of frost carry little bits of the hard material downhill to a pocket where it stops. There, primitive forms of life begin. Sometimes life begins on the rocks themselves, as when moss and lichens team up. The lichens secrete an acid that dissolves little bits of rock; the moss uses this dissolved material as mineral nutrient; it supplies photosynthesis to convert it into proteins and sugars. In time these primitive plants slough off parts or die. The remains of plants and of minute animal life in the degenerated rocks add humus to form soils that support more complex and sophisticated kinds of plants and animal life.

It is said that it takes nature 1,000 years to form an inch of topsoil, and that the world lives on the top six inches of the earth's crust. In fact, that is one way to categorize soils: topsoil and subsoil. Topsoil is mineral soil with a good deal of partially decayed remains (humus) of plants and animals in it. Subsoil is a more mineral undersoil with little or no humus in it. The former is well supplied with air, holds moisture and has many kinds of invisible life in it. The latter doesn't.

3-1. Soil Classifications

Another way to classify soil is by the kind of material that makes it up. Names applied are sandy loam, clay loam and clays.

A useful and official classification by the United States Department of Agriculture provides a picture of the nature of our garden soil. It goes as follows: fine gravel has particles from one to two millimeters in diameter; coarse sands, particles from one-half to one mm.; medium sands, one-quarter to one-half mm.; very fine sands, 5/100 to 1/10 mm.; silts, 5/1000 to 5/100 mm.; clay, 5/1000 mm. and smaller. You'll note that despite the common view of clay soil as being lumpy and cloddy, the individual particles are the smallest of any. More about that later.

In addition, soil may be given textural names with a more practical but less precise description — the kind gardeners can recognize easily. For example, a sandy soil is one in which the individual grains can be seen and felt. If you ball some wet sandy soil in your hands, the ball or wad will break. Such a soil would contain no more than 15 per cent clay and silt.

Coarse sands contain 35 per cent or more coarse sand and fine gravel, and 50 per cent fine or very fine sand. Medium sands contain

Note the differences between (A), a soil low in organic content, and (B), a soil high in organic content.

at least 35 per cent fine gravel and coarse or medium sands, and less than 50 per cent fine sand. Fine sands contain over 50 per cent fine and very fine sands.

Sandy loams hold their shape if squeezed into a ball when wet. In addition to sand, such soils contain from 20 to 50 per cent silt and clay. The group is divided into three subgroups: coarse sandy loams with 45 per cent sand and gravel; medium, with 25 per cent sand and gravel; and fine sandy loams with 50 per cent or more of fine sand.

Loam soils are those that will form a cast even when dry. When wet such soils are runny. They are a relatively even mixture of sand, silt and clay, and have a somewhat gritty feel. Technically, loams contain 20 per cent or less of clay, 30 to 50 per cent silt and 30 to 50 per cent sand.

Silt loams become cloddy or lumpy if they dry out after being wet. They contain 20 per cent or less clay, 50 per cent or more silt, and 50 per cent or less sand. When wet they feel smooth or buttery.

3-2. Most Common Soils

Clay loams are common in North America. They are plastic when wet and can be molded or shaped; they hold that shape as they dry. Clay loams are subdivided into three subgroups: sandy clay loams contain 30 per cent silt and 50 to 80 per cent sand; simple clay loams contain 20 to 50 per cent silt and 20 to 50 per cent sand; silty clay loams contain 30 to 80 per cent silt and less than 30 per cent sand. When wet and squeezed between your fingers it will form a ribbon of soil.

3-3. Clay Soils

Clay soils, the gardener's bugbear, contain 30 per cent or more clay. Sandy clay loams have 50 to 70 per cent sand, 30 to 50 per cent clay and less than 50 per cent silt.

Straight clay loams have less silt and sand. Silty clay loams have 50 to 70 per cent silt and less than 30 per cent sand. Clay soils, 30 per cent or more clay, some silt and some sand, and form a ribbon when squeezed wet. Since clay particles are the smallest, there is less air space. Moreover, these tiny particles adhere to each other very tightly. That's how clay soils produce lumps and clods that make people think they are coarse. It also explains why clay soils, once soaked, stay wet longer; and why, when dry, they shed water. There are few spaces in between the individual particles to allow air and water to enter and leave. And once dried they bake hard with consequent damage to plant roots.

In a way the spaces between the soil particles are like the hole in the doughnut. The space is essential to produce the desired result. In an ideal soil there would probably be 50 per cent space and 50 per cent solids. Again, ideally, the space would be half filled each with water and air.

Another way to describe an ideal soil is to use an old gardener's term — good tilth. This means that the soil is easy to work, lets roots penetrate easily, allows rain to enter freely but does not remain waterlogged, depriving plant roots of air, warms up in spring yet holds moisture in summer. It's obvious then that a garden in good tilth has plenty of spaces between the soil matter that allows a free exchange of air and water.

Creating a garden of good tilth, making a garden of loam should be every home gardener's aim. For although some plants will grow in every kind of soil from dry coarse sands to baked or waterlogged clay, it is only in the garden of good tilth that the lush and productive home garden can exist.

3-4. Organic vs. Inorganic Soils

Going back to the origins of soil, note that the difference between subsoil or primitive soil and topsoil or good gardener's loam was the partly decayed remains of plant and animal

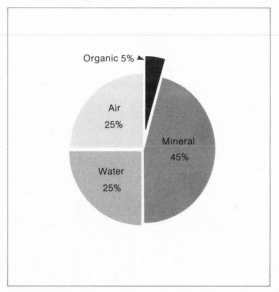

The approximate percentages by volume of water, air, organic matter, and inorganic (mineral) matter in an average soil.

life — humus. In practical terms, a mineral or clay soil depends for its richness on humus. But humus is perishable. In effect it burns up in the soil eventually to produce only the original minerals that went to form the plant or animal. In intensive cultivation, such as a flower or vegetable garden, it burns up more quickly.

Organic matter is probably the single key to improving garden soils no matter what their basic characteristic, sand or clay. Yet in urban gardens it is likely to be in short supply.

Organic additions to soil are often treated mystically, sometimes even referred to as ambrosia. They are credited with providing better human nutrition, longer life, less illness and sometimes even cures for existing illnesses.

Organic additions to garden soils do seem to have magic properties. They enable sandy soil to hold water, break up clay soil, change the color of garden soils so they even look richer, and provide better rooting.

As the humus breaks down, it forms materials that help flocculate clays so that the small aggregates *do* have air and water spaces between them. In the breakdown, humus releases heat and so warms cold soils. It also releases carbon dioxide, an essential plant nutrient. This relatively heavy gas enriches

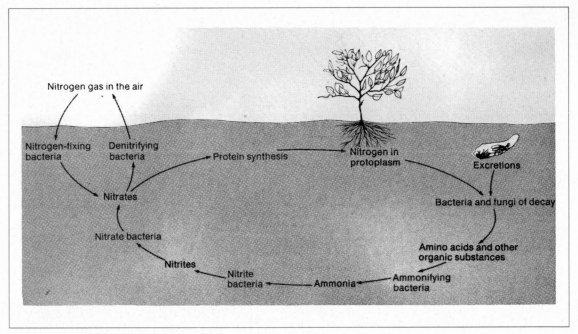

The nitrogen cycle in the soil.

the air around lower leaves and particularly benefits seedlings.

Humus not only holds moisture, it also traps dissolved minerals so that it acts as a food storehouse. It buffers the soil against an alkaline or acid condition for temporary reasons, such as the addition of wood ashes or acid-forming material to the soil. While it tends to warm up cold soils in spring, it helps keep soils cool in summer. And finally, of course, as the breakdown of any one sort of humus is complete, it releases the minerals that originally went into the humus-forming material.

3-5. Up to One-Third Humus

How much humus do you need? A good general rule is to aim for one-third by volume. Many experts agree that an equal parts mixture of gritty sand, sphagnum peat moss and clay loam is ideal. The home gardener should aim for this.

There's another side to the humus story. Soils that are 100 per cent humus are by no means good to garden in. They require manipulation of the water level. And they are deficient in minerals so that virtually all nutrition must come from animal and chemical fertilizers.

Where can you get humus for your garden? The cheapest and simplest source with the kind most likely to have all the nutrients plants require is the home compost pile. Other inexpensive sources are partly-rotted sawdust or wood shavings, leaf mould, bush mould, sewage sludge, and partly-rotted strawy manure or that from bedding made of sawdust. The source will depend on your location. If, for example, you live near a chocolate factory you could use the cocoa bean hulls. We have heard of a gardener who had an instant tea factory nearby — he used composted tea leaves. The same would apply to used coffee grounds from a restaurant.

Commercial sources include dehydrated

*The cheapest source of humus for your garden in the home compost
pile, made partly from leaf mould.*

animal manures (very expensive) and various kinds of peat. Reed and sedge peat is dark brown in color, has considerable nutrients in it, but is short-lived in the soil. So are animal manures — they will last about one year in cultivated soils.

Sphagnum peat moss (peat laid down by the sphagnum moss plants) is virtually worthless as a plant food, but its tough fibers last a long time in the soil. Since it is no fertilizer, it won't interfere with a regular fertilizing program. Sphagnum peat thus is an excellent soil amender for clay and sandy soils alike. In pure sands it should constitute up to 50 per cent of the soil volume. In heavy clays it should be mixed into the soil along with an equal portion of gritty sand. But don't mix sand alone into clay as this produces a kind of cement.

We emphasize mixing sphagum peat *into* the soil. It does not belong on the surface where it will cake after a rain and prevent further water from soaking in. Nor does it belong as top-dressing on a lawn where it will

Unlike most plants, moneywort thrives in acid soil.

form a separate stratum or layer different in texture from the ones below. Again, it belongs under the lawn, mixed into the seed or sod bed.

Dehydrated manures supply a small amount of nutrients and a small amount of humus at an inflated price. They do, however, satisfy a desire on the part of gardeners to use a "natural" fertilizer, although we have never yet met a country gardener who used dehydrated manures. Their advantage over ordinary manure is that they contain no live weed seeds.

3-6. Soil Preparation

Soil preparation should be as deep as you can afford in time, effort and money. Annual flowers and non-root vegetables can often get along on six inches of prepared soil if it is good, and if the unprepared soil underneath is neither impervious nor lying in water. Most plants, however, do better on deeper preparation, unless you have deep topsoil already present. Spring bulbs and lilies need an 18-inch preparation, roses and other shrubs up to three feet, and lawn trees at least as deep. Nor are trees likely to do well where you simply cut a hole in gravel or heavy clay and lay in a pocket of good soil. Subsoils can be broken up by hand digging or by using a pick or a deep plow. If drainage is bad, put in weeping tiles or raise the bed with more soil.

3-7. Acidity and Alkalinity

Many North American soils not on the seacoasts are alkaline and present no problem to the average home vegetable or flower gardens. Many of our favorite plants like alkaline soils. But it does mean you should not apply lime unless a soil test indicates it's necessary. Even then you should probably use gypsum which supplies the lime but is neutral in action, rather than ground agricultural limestone. Never use hydrated lime which can burn.

Where a soil is too alkaline, or where you want to grow acid-soil plants such as blueberries, rhododendrons or azaleas, it may be necessary to change the acid-alkaline reaction. Powdered sulphur acts slowly but over a long period. Sphagnum peat moss, as mentioned, is acid and will help reduce alkalinity of soil when mixed in large proportions with it. Iron sulphate (ferrous) is also acidifying, and at the same time supplies iron to plants in soils where the iron combines with other minerals to form insoluble compounds.

Acid soils are rarer, but occur in pockets and on the coasts. In these areas regular applications of wood ashes or ground limestone or both will keep the soil "sweet" enough to grow most garden plants.

3-8. Sources of Nutrients

The two building materials plants require in the greatest quantities are carbon dioxide (from which they extract the carbon and release the oxygen), and water. The latter is the carrier by which plants take up dissolved minerals; plants use water to store sugar, and water, with carbon and some other minerals, is transformed by the energy of light acting on the chlorophyl in the leaves to make plant sugar and other more complicated materials such as proteins. In general, both carbon dioxide and water are free.

Gardeners usually take this for granted except during droughts when we provide extra water. So that when we talk of plant foods, we are referring to major minerals that are also required for plant growth. These are nitrogen (represented by the symbol N), phosphorus in the form of phosphoric acid (represented by the symbol P) and potassium or potash (represented by the symbol K).

The "Big Three" of plant minerals are available to a limited extent in the soil as it lies unamended. They are also available in varying amounts in home compost or manures.

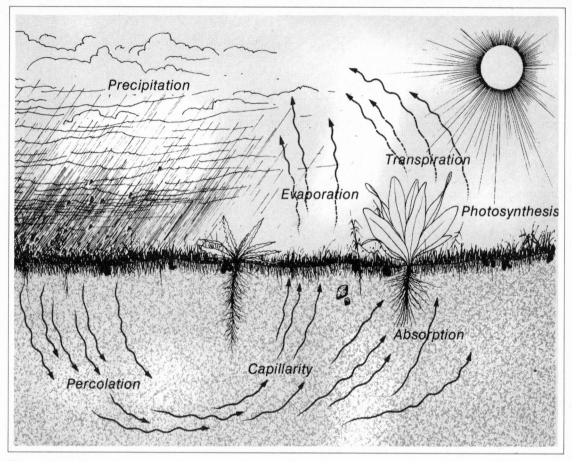

The water cycle.

(Manures are unreliable: they may contain an infinitesimal amount or so much they cause plant burn.)

In fact, almost all forms of decaying plant and animal remains have some fertilizing values. But, exclusively organic gardeners notwithstanding, NPK are available in their cheapest, handiest, and most convenient form as chemical fertilizers. While they do not replace the need for humus, they should be used in conjunction with it.

By law in Canada and in some of the United States fertilizers must specify the percentage of NPK. This is usually expressed as a ratio, such as 10:6:4, 5:10:5, 12:4:8, 4:12:10. In each case the first figure represents N, the second P and the last K.

3-9. What NPK Do

Nitrogen is often the most limiting factor. It boosts leafy and woody growth. It produces deep, dark green leaves. It may also "burn" if applied too liberally. The effect is similar to that of a drought; the solution the roots absorb is too strong and the nitrogen extracts moisture from the plant's tissues.

Phosphorus is also essential to growth, flowering and fruiting, and produces strong tissues. Potassium is needed for cold hardiness, for strong roots and good sap channels in the plant.

Plants cannot use an excess of one element without an adequate amount of the others.

Thus a "complete" fertilizer has some of each of NPK. Nitrogen is the guide element. You judge an application by the amount of N in the fertilizer. The most common measure is to divide the first figure of the fertilizer ratio into 100; use the answer in pounds over 1,000 square feet. This calculation is designed to supply one pound of elemental nitrogen for each 1,000 square feet of garden. Plants that produce a lot of leafy growth, such as grass, deciduous (leaf-shedding) shrubs and trees, corn, lettuce, etc., respond to a fertilizer higher in nitrogen. You still apply one pound of elemental nitrogen per 1,000 square feet, but the ratio of P and K is lower.

3-10. Why Different Fertilizer Ratios?

To give an example, compare a 10:10:10 fertilizer with a 20:10:5. In the first case you'd apply 10 pounds per 1,000 square feet. That would supply one pound of nitrogen, one pound of phosphoric acid and one pound of potash. In the second you'd apply 5 pounds (20 into 100); this would supply one pound of elemental nitrogen, 1/2 pound of phosphoric acid and 1/4 pound of potash.

On the other hand, for root crops, to encourage flowering of shrubs and for lily and spring bulbs, you'd choose a fertilizer higher in P and K. Take one such as 5:10:15. You'd apply 20 pounds (5 into 100) per 1,000 square feet; this would mean one pound of nitrogen, two pounds of phosphoric acid and three pounds of potash. In this way, using chemical fertilizers, you can adjust the relative amounts of the major elements by buying fertilizers with different ratios. This is not possible with organic fertilizers unless you doctor them with chemicals. Don't let the word "chemical" worry you. Most likely the nitrogen came from the air in the first place by nitrogen fixation plants; the phosphorus from acid-treated rock and the potash from old sea beds in Saskatchewan, not all that unnatural.

In fact, all plant fertilizers are based on the elemental minerals. Plants can't eat and so you can't feed them. What plants can do is take up moisture from the soil in which there are dissolved minerals. As water evaporates from the leaf surface, more is taken up through the sap channels from the roots to replace it — a tree may be thought of as a column of water from roots to topmost leaf, the leaves acting like a pump at the top of a well. This is why growth is fastest in warm weather with adequate soil moisture: leaves evaporate water faster.

Thus, whether organic or inorganic, the tissue-building minerals have to be in elemental form, dissolved in water, to be used. If they are, the plant can't tell the difference — nor can a laboratory — whether they came from manure or from a fertilizer factory.

3-11. What Trace Elements Are

Plants also need other elements such as iron, copper, boron, manganese, copper, zinc, in much smaller quantities, sometimes in minute traces. These other minerals are called "trace elements". They may be applied by chemical mixture if there is a deficiency in your soil. This is unlikely, however, and in most cases, additions of humus-forming materials will supply all that are necessary. Home compost with orange peels from Florida or California, pineapple peelings from Hawaii, potato peelings from Prince Edward Island or Idaho, and so forth, will likely contain all the trace elements any plant needs. If in doubt, or if your plants show signs of a deficiency, have your soil tested by the department of agriculture or a commercial laboratory, or do your own testing with a kit, regarding the results only as a general guide.

In general it is better to supply a little less fertilizer than your plants need rather than too much. If your soil is naturally rich and your plants grow satisfactorily with the addition of some compost annually, you may not need additional fertilizer at all.

When using dry, bagged fertilizer, you can incorporate it with the soil when preparing lawn seedbeds, vegetable and flower gardens, and bulb beds, hedge planting areas or foundation evergreen beds. Dry fertilizer should not come into contact with plant roots or other parts as it draws moisture from them. It may also be broadcast evenly over the surface as for lawns. Incorporate it into the top inch of soil around trees and shrubs, between annuals or rows of vegetables. Then water it in.

3-12. How to Use Concentrates

Chemical fertilizers also come in concentrated forms at very high prices. These are completely soluble and bear ratios such as 20:20:20, 15:30:15, 10:52:17. Many also contain small amounts of trace elements. These should never be used dry but only in a water solution. The standard dilution rate is one teaspoon per quart of water or a rounded tablespoon per gallon. They are best used to settle in new transplants or for container plants.

Over the summer use them in place of normal watering once every week to 10 days. Their effect is immediate and fleeting.

By understanding how the soil works, you can change its texture and increase the nutrients available so your plants are more rewarding. It is always easier in the long run to amend the soil before you plant than to try to do it from the surface down in the years to come.

Elements of Landscaping: Trees, Shrubs, Lawns, Flowers and Vines

When we notice the grounds around a house, we can tell immediately if they flatter the house. We probably also note a prominent feature — a blue spruce, flowering bulbs in spring, bright annuals in summer, a flowering shrub or a tree that colors brightly in fall.

We do not usually dissect the planting around the house or in the back garden to note specifically that that is a deciduous tree, or this a spring-flowering shrub. We may notice that the grass is thin and pale or rich green and lush, but we don't note to ourselves just how that deep green flatters the shrubs and ties the house to the grounds (although we may occasionally observe that a thin, weedy lawn makes the house itself look somehow shabby and rundown). Nevertheless it is obvious when you think about it that the whole picture of house and garden is made up of a number of different plants. Trees alone can't produce that landscaping. Nor can annual flowers, shrubs or evergreens alone.

Sometimes it is useful to separate a garden into such distinct elements if only to understand what function they perform. By knowing the growing habits and the flower characteristics, the foliage color, shape and texture, and the ultimate height and spread of all the various kinds of plants available to us, we stand a much better chance of arranging a planting that satisfies our needs, as we discussed in Chapters 1 and 2.

4-1. What Is a Tree?

The concept of a tree seems so obvious that it may seem silly to ask what it is. But it's surprising to find how few people can come up with a ready definition. Most of us have a picture of a full-grown tree in a park in mind, but do not relate the concept of a tree to a home garden.

To start, of course, we all know that trees come in two basic divisions, deciduous (leaf-shedding) and evergreen (leaves drop, but not all at once, so there are always some leaves on the tree). We tend to think of deciduous trees as broad-leafed and evergreens as needle-leafed. However, there are broad-leafed kinds that are evergreen, such as the live or evergreen oak, the arbutus tree, citrus and olives, etc. And there are needle-leafed trees or conifers that are deciduous. Examples are larches (tamarack), bald cypress, dawn redwood.

Another definition of a tree is by the shade it gives. Usually by shade tree we mean a broad-leafed deciduous plant that does not lose its attractiveness if we remove its lower branches so that we can use the space under it, meanwhile being shaded from the summer sun. The conifers, too, can be pruned of branches high up on the trunk, as happens naturally in a forest, but for garden purposes such pruning ruins the appearance we seek in

Common evergreen trees.

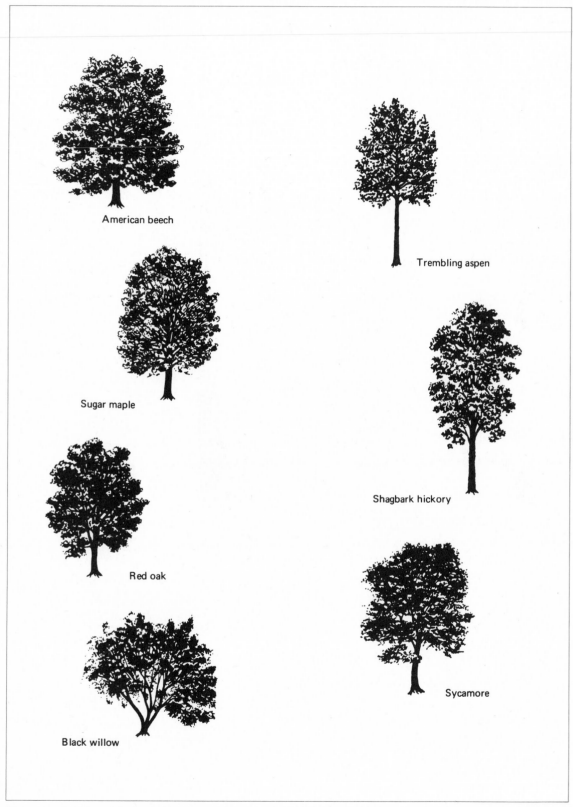

American beech

Trembling aspen

Sugar maple

Shagbark hickory

Red oak

Black willow

Sycamore

Common deciduous trees.

*The beginning gardener must be careful to plant trees that will be the right
size for his property when they become full-grown.*

them. A perfect blue spruce is one that you
can't walk or sit under — its lower branches,
still well-clothed in needles, sweep the
ground to make an almost perfect cone from
there to the growing tip.

Within the range of broad-leafed shade
trees, there is a wide variation and the
gardener should know what he wants before
planting. Even within plant families there is
wide variance. Acer, the maple family, offers
many fine trees, but not all are suitable to
every garden. The magnificent sugar maple
will grow up to 120 feet tall, with a huge,
spreading ball-shaped head that provides
dense shade underneath. Its roots, like those
of other trees, will spread out from the trunk as
far as the branches spread. And most of the
feeder roots are concentrated within the top
six inches of soil. One mature sugar maple will
occupy more than one small city lot, and
make it virtually impossible to grow anything
else.

In contrast, the Amur river maple *(Acer
ginnala)* grows to a maximum of 20 feet. It,
too, has bright fall leaf color, but doesn't
dominate a small yard. Moreover it is hardy in
the dry air and cold winters of the midwest
where the sugar maple won't grow. The Amur
maple is sometimes available at nurseries as
a shrub. This brings up another garden
definition of a tree: a woody, perennial plant
that has one central trunk. In many cases the
home gardener (and the nurseryman) can
grow a specific plant as either a shrub or a
tree depending on whether it is allowed to
develop more than one main stem. The
distinction is not really artificial since many
"trees" develop sucker shoots about the base
that would eventually become trunks; many
shrubs have a tendency to produce one shoot
that is stronger than the rest.

The picture is further complicated by the
fact that we like to grow some trees with more
than one stem. Paper birch are the classic

In areas where winter stops all outdoor plant growth, a basement plant room offers pleasing color.

Unlike most trees, the paper birch is valued for its multi-stemmed clumps.

example where multi-stemmed clumps are valued for decorative purposes. Here the difference is between youth and age. When mature, the birch clump becomes a multi-stemmed tree.

Basically we can think of a tree as a woody, perennial plant that has one central trunk that branches well above the ground. Besides giving cooling shade to sit under, it helps cool the street, the garden and the house by intercepting the sun and by the evaporation of water from its leaves. In practical terms, even if you have no feeling for trees themselves, they are nature's air conditioner, and make a mechanical air conditioner more efficient. A tree shading a house wall or roof can save hundreds of dollars worth of electricity. Trees also help filter traffic noises and street sounds, and trap some pollution in the air.

It is for its looks, however, that most of us want a tree in our gardens. It softens the lines of the house and helps make it seem a part of the landscape. Planted to one side of a tall narrow house, it makes it seem wider and less like an obelisk. Its green leaves add a cool color to summer, and its overhead branches provide a roof for the outdoor living area. No engineered piece of gym equipment is half as attractive to pre-teen children as a tree with branches strategically placed for climbing.

By choosing for his own preference, a gardener can get more than all these values from a tree. Some have outstanding flowers (flowering crabapples, flowering cherries,

Chinese pagoda tree, magnolia, horse chestnut). Some have outstanding fall leaf color (sugar and red maple, red oak, pin oak, paper birch, cherries, yellowwood, beech). Some have particularly beautiful winter forms (Japanese tree lilac, ash). And there is an occasional tree that combines a number of seasons' interests. Examples are the mountain ash with white flowers, colorful fruit and red fall leaf color; the paper birch; and the swamp red maple with small red flowers in spring, bright fall leaf color and red twigs in winter.

4-2. Evergreen Trees

As we've noted, needle evergreen trees seldom make good shade trees. But they have another function: they are the mainstay of the garden foliage all year long. Their usually sombre greens are the background for the deciduous trees and shrubs in summer, and the focal point in the winter. Thus they are the garden anchors around which you can build the rest of the planting. They are often very decorative in themselves and may be used as

A blue spruce in a container can be a Christmas tree in winter and a patio decoration in summer.

specimen trees to decorate a lawn or set off the architecture of the house. Their foliage colors vary from the dark, almost black green of Austrian pines, through the Japanese yews and the old needles of Colorado blue spruce, and the grass green of Alberta spruce, to the blue of Blue Haven Juniper and the near silver of Hoopsi blue spruce. Heights vary from six to 10 feet for the Dwarf Alberta conical spruce, through 10 to 12 feet for an old Japanese yew to 90 feet or more for full-size spruce and pines.

When planting evergreen trees anywhere near a house, remember that their foliage is there in winter when the days are short and the weather dull as well as in summer when light is intense and the days long. Don't plant them too close to house doors and windows.

4-3. Shrubs and Their Uses

Deciduous shrubs may be the most versatile group of plants in the garden. Varying in height from barely inches to 15 or 20 feet, they can offer something for every garden from minuscule to grand. There are kinds with special bloom qualities such as lilacs, forsythias, flowering almonds and tree peony (spring), spirea and mock orange (June-July), hydrangea (summer), summer spirea and Rose of Sharon (late summer) that make having them worthwhile even though they may not have decorative qualities you admire at other times of the year.

Some, like spice viburnum and spice bush (and lilacs), are valuable for their perfume alone. Still others offer brilliant fall color (spindle or burning bush, sumac, high bush blueberry, azalea). Some have colored foliage or leaves with two or more colors (silverleaf dogwood, Emerald Gaiety euonymus, golden privet, golden mock orange, Shubert purple chokecherry, purple sand cherry). Others bear fruit such as currants, gooseberries, serviceberries, high bush cranberries (which also have white flowers and red

Syringa vulgaris hybrids make a large, fragrant hardy shrub for northern gardens.

Most deciduous shrubs should not be pruned to form round globes, but have a few branches removed to the ground.

leaves in fall), bush roses (for rose hip jam and wine). Others bear fruit that, while not useful to us, is attractive to the eye or to wildlife (honeysuckle, coral berry, bush rose, buffalo berry, sumac).

Almost all shrubs lend themselves to providing privacy and some special ones to hedging since they take clipping very well — see Chapter 9 on hedges. They are virtually self-maintaining once established. By choosing kinds that bloom at various times over the growing season you can have something in bloom until after killing frost when witch hazel opens its yellow flowers, without the maintenance that a flower garden requires. It is hard to imagine a garden without shrubs.

4-4. Evergreen Shrubs

Dwarf needle evergreens and needle evergreen shrubs are not nearly so colorful as deciduous shrubs, but like their taller-growing cousins, they clothe our gardens in winter when many deciduous shrubs look like dead sticks. And for that we can forgive them their lack of spectacular flowers.

We distinguish between dwarf versions of larger trees, such as miniature junipers and pines, nest spruce and globe or dwarf blue spruce, and those kinds that naturally grow shrubby, such as the many low, medium and relatively tall-growing junipers.

Many gardeners buy young plants of Pfitzer juniper, for example, with the idea it will forever fit into a small space near the foundation wall. Without pruning, such plants will eventually grow 12 feet tall and nearly as big across. Similarly, mugho ball pines, unless sheared annually, will grow tall enough eventually to make a hiding spot for children playing games. There are ground-covering evergreens, such as rug junipers, including the new Gardens Canada Blue and Green Acres, that supply a decorative answer to many garden problems. They literally cover

Springbank Juniper

Skyrocket Juniper

Meyer's Juniper

Blue Heaven Juniper

the ground with attractive foliage between other larger plants or around deciduous trees and shrubs; they can be used to plant banks and so suppress weeds and prevent erosion where the slope is too great to make mowing (or even growing) grass practical. They will grow on dry, exposed sites where few other plants will do well.

Intermediate-size evergreens such as hybrid yews, spreading junipers and dwarf mugho pines bridge the gap between the very low growers and full-size evergreens. Planted in a pleasing arrangement — spreading kinds by windows, upright types by house corners or near upright beams or walls of brick — they do the same for structures as they do for large trees: bridge the gap between the horizontal line of the soil at the foundation and the upright lines of the building. Hence the name "foundation planting".

4-5. Broad-Leafed Evergreen Shrubs

Just as there are broad-leafed evergreen trees, so there are similar shrubs. And while the list of those that are hardy in northern climates is small, it does include more kinds than the list of broad-leafed evergreen trees. One kind is quite hardy indeed and will survive in the midwest — Korean boxwood. Other relatively hardy kinds include the Oregon grape holly *(Mahonia aquifolium)*, Julian barberry, firethorn and evergreen euonymus *(U-on-i-muss)* such as the Emerald Gaiety mentioned earlier. These plants may be grown (and trimmed to shape) in the foundation planting, in a mixed shrub and evergreen grouping, or as low to medium hedges. Firethorn can be trained against a wall, as may some of the upright euonymuses. In areas with mild winters (and below the snowline) they will remain evergreen. In both severe and snowless winters they will drop their leaves but produce new ones in spring. Their advantage is in the different texture of their flat leaves as a contrast to

needle evergreens and the leafless deciduous shrubs. In addition, the grape holly has bronzy-red, holly-like leaves and the same fall and winter color, yellow flowers and black, grape-like fruit. The firethorn has white flowers and bright red berries, as have many kinds of euonymus. All will grow in ordinary garden soils without special preparation, but remain in better shape through winter and spring with wind and sun protection, especially in March when the ground is frozen but the sun and wind strong.

There is another group of broad-leafed evergreen plants valuable for their flowers or fruit that requires special soil conditions — acid and very humusy, though well-drained. These include rhododendrons (and azaleas), holly, leucothoe, andromeda, heath and heathers. They are also rather frost-tender and grow best on the east and west coasts and in the southern United States, although they can be quite successful in colder areas with proper soil preparation and sun and wind protection. Holly does well on the coast of British Columbia, in the Pacific northwest, in southern New England, and in certain areas of the U.S. South.

All these woody, perennial plants, trees, shrubs and evergreens are the more or less permanent framework of your garden, with one addition — the lawn.

4-6. The Lawn

If trees, shrubs and evergreens are the garden framework, its background or the bridge between soil line and house architecture, the lawn is the foreground and the playground of the garden. It is not always easy to grow and to maintain good grass — in some cases, such as in dense city shade, it may be impossible — but few of us would like to have grounds around a house without at least a patch of green grass.

We inherited many of our ideas of what gardens should be from English gardening. In that rainy country it is relatively easy to grow good grass. However, continental climates like ours do not provide sufficient rainfall in the middle of the growing season, nor do they stay cool enough in summer in most areas for grass to thrive without a good deal of help from us. Nevertheless there are few ground covers as versatile, as easy to maintain and as tolerant of foot traffic as lawn grasses. And when well maintained there are few things you can grow that are as nice to walk on in bare feet, as cool-looking in summer, and that provide as rich a foreground to your house.

Plant breeders are coming to our rescue with new selections and even true hybrids that stand deep freezing well in winter, that are more drought resistant, and that will grow without the heavy fertilization that the first luxury grasses required. Besides looking cool, vigorously growing grass actually does cool the air around it by giving off moisture, and improves it by absorbing carbon dioxide

and giving off oxygen during the daylight hours. It is the first of our plants to show green color in spring and the last to give it up in fall or winter, often showing up green during a thaw in winter.

In the same practical vein, lawn grasses with their fibrous and interwoven roots are first-rate soil holders and thus a valuable tool in preventing erosion on banks and slopes where the grade is not too steep to prevent mowing. And where growth is stimulated by proper maintenance, grasses will improve the soil they grow in — it was the prairie grasses over myriad years that built the rich, deep topsoil there.

Lawns are, of course, made up of a large number of rather small plants. As a result it is very easy to tailor the size of the turf to the property. There are lawns as small as two feet square between paving stones on tiny city

Geraniums and dusty miller are ideal flowers for a spot garden.

The purple grape hyacinth here provides a bright border for multi-colored tulips. (Photo by Malak)

yards, and as large as several acres on large suburban or rural properties. One apartment garden we visited had little squares of "lawn" carefully nurtured in wooden boxes to provide the foreground and green color for a potted tree.

4-7. Flowers: Low or High

By garden flowers, most people do not mean flowers on trees and shrubs, although, of course, flowering shrubs and trees add their own color in season. But these are at a high level and most gardeners think of flowers as low plants with color near the ground. In fact you could say that to most people, summer flowers mean those plants they buy in flats, pots or boxes in spring to transplant into the ground in special areas or among shrubs and evergreens, and which flower from the time of purchase till killing frost. These plants are mainly summer annual flowers (or behave like summer annuals). They grow from seed to flowering in one season and must be replaced each year. They are easy to grow, relatively cheap, quick and probably provide more color for the money than anything else. They are especially valuable in new gardens where there are few other things planted, or where the other plants are young. They can be massed in beds, used to fill spots where shrubs and evergreens will be planted, grown in patio or balcony containers, window boxes, near paths and doorways without fear they will overrun their space (even if they do, slightly, they die off with frost, anyway).

Annuals can be planted massed, all of a kind, mixed with different members of the same family for a color or height contrast, arranged with other annuals from low, ground-hugging ones such as sweet alyssum, ageratum or portulaca to three-foot or higher zinnias and marigolds. You could use these tall plants as a background next to a fence or sunny wall, or you could use them in the centre of a bed with lower-growing kinds

Foxglove is a biennial that is sometimes treated as an annual.

arranged in tiers back down to ground level on both sides and ends of the planting.

As stated previously, annuals are most easily bought as started plants in flower or ready to bloom. In colder areas they may also be started at home from seed in mid to late March if you have a bright, but cool growing area, or outdoors where they are to bloom.

Some plants are treated like annuals although they are really tender perennials. These include coleus, grown for its bright leaf color, impatiens which is excellent in shade, wax begonias for part shade, full sun, pots, boxes and massing or mixing, and the old favorite geranium which can be used alone, to fill in bare spots — anywhere there is sun. Like annuals, this group can be bought as started plants. They can also be started by rooting cuttings in sand and peat or vermiculite, and in this way new plants started in late summer can be carried over winter to provide new cuttings for next summer's garden. They may also be started from seed indoors in late winter.

Other plants sometimes treated as annuals are really biennials. Examples include pansy, pinks, sweet william, forget-me-nots, foxglove, canterbury bells. Grown as biennials, they are started from seed one summer to produce young plants by fall. Their roots live over winter, sprout in spring and produce flowers. Many biennials can be treated as long-season annuals: start the seed early enough indoors and they'll bloom the first season. They may also be bought as started plants. And many of them, especially pansy and forget-me-not, will self-seed and produce their own young plants in fall for next year's bloom, although the quality may run down in this way.

Still other popular garden flowers are perennials. These include peonies, garden iris, delphiniums, phlox, chrysanthemums (where hardy), carnations (where hardy), oriental poppy and many others. Generally these plants will last for many years. While some tend to die out and will need replacing, others, like peonies, may be blooming as well 75 years later as they do now. Others, like iris, multiply quickly and need dividing frequently.

Perennials behave much like flowering shrubs in terms of their garden value (although of course they die back to the ground each winter while shrubs don't). They bloom mostly just once during the season (delphiniums will bloom twice if cut down, fertilized and watered after the first flowering), but obviously don't have to be replaced each year.

Perennials can be started from seed although this is much too lengthy a procedure for most home gardeners, especially for peonies. Others may be worth it; delphiniums, for example, will usually bloom the second year after sowing; carnations and dahlias the first year if started early enough indoors. But

Where hardy, chrysanthemums are a popular perennial.

Double-flowered gloriosa was developed from the black-eyed Susan, a wildflower.

Day lilies bloom at various times from spring to fall.

most of us will buy root divisions or started plants from plant sales stations or nurseries.

Other summer flowers grow from tender summer bulbs. These include tuberous begonias, caladiums (for colored leaves), dahlias, gladiolus, canna lily. If you live in an area that is not frost-free, they must be taken up each fall, stored and then replanted the next year. But because they can be stored indoors each winter, and because some tend to multiply rather well, they represent good value for the gardener. The tender summer bulbs are available in bins and packages for starting yourself. Some may be available as started plants. These include tuberous begonias, canna lilies and caladiums.

Finally, there are two groups of hardy bulbs which are perennial: lilies which bloom in summer and fall, and the spring bulbs which bloom in early to late spring. The former include old standby types, but if you are buying new bulbs, look to some of the newer hybrids produced in Oregon. These include Midcentury and Harlequin hybrids, Olympic hybrids and speciosum hybrids that produce more spectacular flowers than lilies ever had before. Lilies are available as dry bulbs in packages in late fall (and occasionally in spring). They may arrive late so planting holes should be prepared before the ground surface is likely to freeze in your area (cover any such holes so they don't present any hazard).

Lilies can add an exotic or spectacular touch of color and perfume to the summer garden. Various kinds bloom from early summer through fall but they only bloom once, so treat them as you would herbaceous perennials. Build the rest of the flowering garden around them, or plant different kinds of lilies and other perennials so there is a succession of bloom.

Modern lilies are relatively free of disease, and quite hardy — some have been developed on the Canadian prairies. They do, however, need well-drained soil and regular fertilizing; otherwise they tend to fade out. Plant them

Gladiolus is perhaps the most commonly planted tender summer bulb; it must be dug up, cleaned and stored in a dark room during winter. (Photo by Malak)

The Imperial Crimson lily grows to heights of three feet and must be tied to a stake for support.

Unlike most lilies, the Madonna lily (shown above with delphiniums in the background) has shallow roots. Generally, lilies are deep-rooted.

Tulips are popular for the bright colors they provide in mid-spring. (Photo by Malak)

Among hardy spring-flowering bulbs are the early daffodil, the Praestans Fusileer tulip and the tiny glory-of-the-snow. (Photo by Malak)

where they get dappled sun or light shade in the afternoon so their colors will hold and the flowers will last. Since they are mostly tall-growing — up to three feet or more — they look best when planted as a background, or in a clump to be seen from a distance, or against a fence with lower-growing perennials or annuals in front. Lilies root deeply (except for Madonna lilies) and the shallow-rooted annuals do not compete for root space. But, like most other plants, lilies will not compete with pervasive-rooted trees, shrubs and evergreens.

4-8. The Spring Bulbs

Most gardeners are aware of the spring-flowering hardy bulbs and admire them in other people's yards or in public parks. Every spring they vow to have tulips, daffodils, hyacinths and the small bulbs — crocuses, squills, grape hyacinths, snowflakes and glory-of-the-snow — blooming in their yards by the next season. The trouble is that spring-flowering hardy bulbs must be planted at least six weeks before freeze-up. This means working in the garden when the nights are drawing in and the weather is often unpleasant. Unfortunately there is no way yet of planting this group in the spring for flowering the same year. So it's well worth the effort to plan spring bulb plantings, order the bulbs in late summer, and then get out and dig in fall.

Chosen from among the small bulbs that bloom early, and from the various classes of tulips and daffodils, plus hyacinths where hardy, a spring bulb planting can produce up to 10 weeks of bloom, starting from when the snow first goes until late May or early June

Crocuses are among the earliest flowers to appear in early spring. (Photo by Malak)

when the herbaceous perennials start to bloom.

Tulips and hyacinths can be planted in blocks to form a sheet of color, in small groups of three to nine bulbs to form a spot of color, or in undulating patterns. It is no longer stylish to plant large formal beds as is still done in public parks and display gardens; the cost and the labor are too great for the home gardener who does all his or her own labor. Instead, plant groups of these bulbs (and of daffodils) against a south wall for early color among later-blooming perennials, among evergreens where there are gaps, in an annual flower bed where deeply-planted tulips and daffodils can remain all year and not interfere with the annuals that you can plant between the bulbs' foliage. The annuals expand to fill the flower beds as bulb foliage matures, turns brown and dies. Their bloom hides the browning bulb foliage.

Small groups of bulbs brighten foundation plantings near building walls. Their cheery flowers brighten the planting before new growth appears on the evergreens. Set out summer flowering bulbs mentioned earlier for summer color when the spring bulbs have faded.

Hyacinths are more formal and thus look better in slightly formal planting patterns. They are highly perfumed and extra nice near a doorway or by the patio so you can smell them when sitting out on a warm spring day. The little bulbs can be set in almost any small pocket of cultivated soil in the yard. They do well in a rock garden, at the edge of another kind of garden such as a rose garden, mixed with larger bulbs such as early tulips or daffodils, in a wild or natural garden, or in massed planting in the cultivated area around trees. Siberian squills are particularly effective this way. They multiply rapidly and soon produce a carpet of blue in early spring.

Crocuses can even co-exist with grass providing it isn't mowed too low or too soon in spring. They also look very good around deciduous shrubs where they can achieve their growth before the shrub comes into leaf. In the same way, daffodils can be planted under high-branched but deep-rooted deciduous trees. Daffodils will also do well near

streams and lakes and if planted in an informal pattern, appear natural or native. This kind of planting is known as "naturalizing".

For most effective use of spring bulbs, make each small grouping of the same named variety bulb. Don't mix up different classes of tulips. There are very early, early, mid-season and late-blooming classes of tulips; each class has many named varieties, each with different heights, colors and blooming times. If each group of three, seven or nine bulbs you plant is the same named variety, they'll bloom at the same time and with the same color. You can get contrast by planting a different variety in a small cluster nearby.

4-9. Vines

There are a number of unrelated plants with climbing habits that we might also consider under the many other categories we've discussed: vines. There are annual and perennial kinds, evergreen and deciduous. But the fact they climb makes it tempting to lump them all together, from the annual morning glory to the evergreen perennial honeysuckle.

Perhaps the most commonly planted kinds of vine are evergreen English ivy and Boston ivy or Virginia creeper. These plants can cling to masonry or wood structures and are valued because they give a soft, green look to the area they occupy, and cool the structure behind. Some gardeners worry that they will damage the mortar between bricks, which they may do ultimately, but you only need to look at some of the ancient vines on even older masonry walls in Europe to realize it won't disintegrate in your lifetime.

Climbing plants occupy little root space for the foliage cover they provide and so are very useful on small properties. They take the flowers up to and past eye level, as with clematis and honeysuckle. They can decorate a wall, as we've seen, a fence post or a patio. They can even provide food as scarlet runner beans and grapes do.

Wisteria, which starts out as a vine, eventually develops a trunk that is self-supporting. It produces long, vigorous shoots each year and needs severe trimming to keep it in bounds. For the first years at least, it should have stakes, a trellis or other firm support. It can be used beside a house wall, a trellis, patio roof or garden arbor.

4-10. Others to Use as Climbers

There are other plants that can be used in your landscaping in a similar manner. The first and most common are so-called climbing roses. Roses don't really climb. What they do is grow long, arching canes that will in fact trail if left alone. But by fastening them to supports we gain the effect of a vining plant. Fruit trees and ornamental shrubs and trees may be trained the same way by judicious (and continual) pruning to give them artificial shapes such as fan, U, double-U and horizontal (cordons).

These trained (sometimes called "espaliered") trees or shrubs can perform several functions. The most obvious is that of wall or fence decoration. Trained trees almost always draw exclamations from visitors and are a source of pride to the gardener. They make it possible to grow fruit in very small planting areas that would not accommodate a tree allowed to develop a full, natural top. And by taking advantage of the warmth absorbed from house walls, they can ripen fruit in climates colder than normal for the kind of fruit.

With decorative trees and shrubs such as juniper and firethorn, they add attractive foliage or fruit color or both to the house wall. They are, however, considerably more demanding of the gardener: as mentioned, they must be pruned frequently and not allowed to "get away" on you. They need more careful attention to watering and fertilizing. They may need frequent spraying (apples, crabs, roses especially, but also other fruit) and this could lead to discoloration, especially of painted wood surfaces.

There are also other kinds of plants or plant groupings of interest mainly to the specialist or devoted hobbyist. These include alpine plants, wildflowers, and swamp and bog gardens with the plants suitable to that environment.

4-11. Bringing It All Together

We have discussed many categories of plants and their uses in the home garden. This is not to say that every garden should have one or more of each of them. In most cases the result would be a jungle that you couldn't walk in, let alone tell one plant from another.

As suggested in Chapter 2, the idea is to decide what you want from your garden and what kind of picture you want to create. Then go over all the kinds of effects you can achieve with the possibilities mentioned in this chapter. Check with local nurserymen as to species and varieties suitable to your climate and soil, and start painting your own garden picture.

Elements of Landscaping: Space, Grade, Color, Water

5-1. Space

Repeated references have been made to the garden picture that you create with good plantings. But the references are misleading, for a picture is really only a flat image of one dimension. Our minds supply the depth from the shadings, color changes and foreshortening provided by the camera or the artist.

Not so in the garden. There we are dealing with genuine depth and we have to take it into account when we lay out the garden and set out the plants. Take an obvious example. A three- or four-foot-high spreading juniper might appear completely inadequate and seem to be growing in the wrong direction when planted at the house corner. Yet planted at the edge of the patio where people are seated, it might be too high to see over.

Another example would be the proper use of a tall, thin plant such as Skyrocket juniper. This attractive, blue-foliaged evergreen grows in the form of a narrow cone, the base never more than a few feet across. But it may reach heights of 30 feet or more. Its proportions and the space it occupies make it seem unnatural when surrounded by nothing but lawn or when its height dominates a low building. The depth proportion returns, however, when it is planted in a row as a property divider, or when marking upright columns of a tall building.

In a similar way, ball-shaped plants (or those trimmed that way) tend to make everything on the property look smaller if they are planted alone as specimens on a lawn. A taller-growing plant left unclipped provides a better proportion. We expect trees to be tall. However, that same ball plant might supply just the rounded shape necessary to take away from the angularity of a fence post, or to mark the entrance way along a path, or as part of a mixed evergreen planting, perhaps with a Skyrocket juniper in the center.

So the depth or the proportions of the volume of space occupied by a plant must be considered in relation to other plants, the structures on the property and the size of the garden. Space and depth should also be considered in relation to the whole garden, front or back. And it is here that a seeming contradiction lies. A small garden devoted entirely to grass without marking off boundaries appears smaller. On the other hand, if the garden areas are defined by various plantings, the eye comes to a stop at some point — the property line. If the plantings are at each side so that there are points of interest along the way, but still allow a full sweep of the length, the illusion of distance is created.

One way to increase this feeling is to use low-growing, dwarf plants in beds along the length. Another is to use an oval planting with the points of the oval on the longest dimension of the property. The grass could occupy

Espalier adapted to five-in-one apple on variable-height fence.

the center of the oval shape with shrubs, evergreens, flower and bulb beds filling in the rectangular limits of the property, and giving the grass its oval shape. From the patio, or inside the house, the lawn and garden appear to be in fact oval, and that shape gives a greater illusion of distance and depth than if the grass line followed the rectangular property line.

On a larger property you can achieve a

greater illusion of depth and space by separating off sections of the garden so the entrance way and just a tantalizing glimpse of a partly-hidden garden "room" can be seen from the house or patio. The eye picks up the separation; the mind fills in the picture with the idea of a space beyond.

A winding garden path that passes out of sight beyond a planting such as some shrubs or moderate sized evergreens, and then winds back into view later when it will appear narrower and further away, lends a great deal more depth to the garden and an illusion of far greater space than if the same path went straight from back step to property line.

On tiny lots such as those belonging to houses in downtown cores, it is not really possible to do very much in a linear way to extend the feeling of depth from door to property line. But it is possible to expand the feeling of space by extending the garden upward — use the air space and create a garden 1-1/2 storeys high.

A high board or palisade type of fence made with vertical cedar poles can be built to 15 or 20 feet. Plants can be trained to the house wall and to the fence so they grow vertical and flat as discussed in the previous chapter. Hanging baskets of plants can be fastened at various heights to the fence. You may have no vista at all when sitting out in this kind of garden, but it achieves an open-top quality that helps make up for its postage stamp size.

One caution about trying to get the illusion of space at the expense of trying to use the garden: it is tempting to have tiny walks and paved areas that are too small in order to make the grass and planting areas larger. Every time you enter, leave or sit out, you feel squeezed. The effect would be much more agreeable with a large, welcoming path, and a patio at least large enough to accommodate several guests comfortably, even though it meant cutting down the grassed area.

You may be able to gain space another way. Instead of cutting the yard in two with large paving stones or concrete, run the path to the driveway from the side of the porch or steps. Or use stepping stones (or wood

rounds) set into the ground with grass growing between.

5-2. Grade

One of the obvious ways of dealing with absolutely flat land where doors and windows face directly onto the street is to create artificial hills with soil brought in close to the street line. This adds an interesting, undulating line to the landscape, helps screen street noises and provides privacy for the tenants. This illustrates just how important the grade of the land is to the look of the complete garden.

A change in grade adds interest to any landscape. Few of us like looking at absolutely flat land, yet that is what most of us have to deal with. Unfortunately too many of us take the easy way out — simply lay sod over that flatness. Even with a gentle slope, we tend to follow that same easy way out. With a little effort, though, we could change the grade more dramatically in one area, still using the same total volume of soil. Examples of this technique are terraces, banks, hummocks and raised planting beds.

If your property slopes from the house gently down to the property line, by gathering earth from the lower level and placing it on the area closer to the house where the patio is, you can create a two-level garden, perhaps with stones, wood rounds or sawn-up timbers as steps leading below. Or the soil could be piled to one corner giving a different effect and a drop that could be used to create a small waterfall. The only restraint is the amount of work needed, and the need to allow for drainage. In most areas it is illegal to change the grade of your property so as to block the natural watercourse. In other words, you must not build up the height of your land to block the natural drainage of your neighbor's, or cause your run-off water to flood his land when it didn't before. If this seems likely to happen as a result of your regrading, use weeping tiles under the built-up soil to take care of drainage.

Even if it doesn't seem practical to you to have rolling hills or a terrace, and you would still like to add a grade change to your yard, consider a level but raised planting bed. Simply build a low retaining wall of stone, brick, horizontal or vertical logs, and fill topsoil in behind, bearing in mind the admonition about changing your neighbor's drainage. Such a raised planting bed at the end of the property could raise a flower bed to eye level, making it visible from the patio and adding an attraction to draw the eye down the length of the yard. It also has some very practical values, as anyone with a bad back will tell you. A raised bed makes planting, weeding and watering much easier. It also solves the problem of trying to grow plants, particularly roses, in a badly drained area. By raising the bed you automatically improve the drainage drastically.

A word of warning, though, about changing the grade of land over the roots of trees: most trees have adjusted their feeding roots' height to suit them exactly the way things are. If you fill earth over them to a depth of more than

A garden planted on different levels of grade adds interest to the landscape.

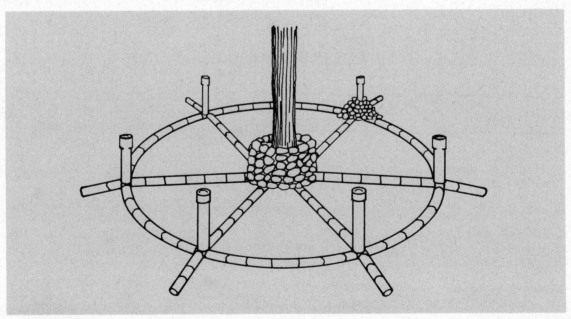

To protect tree roots when you change the level of the grade, place red clay weeping tiles in the form of a wagon wheel around the trunk. The tiles should extend as far out as the branch spread.

one or two inches, you prevent air from reaching them and they may die. On the other hand, if you scrape the soil away from over the roots, you expose them to heat and drying which will also have a damaging effect on them.

There are some partial remedies. You can build a stone or brick well around the tree trunk, out as far as the branch spread, to hold the earth fill back and so keep the grade the same. Another method is to run a series of red clay weeping tiles like the spikes of a wagon wheel out from the trunk and in a circle around the outside like the tire of the wheel. Interconnected with these should be tiles set vertically to allow air to enter. Conversely if you are taking earth away, leave the soil as it is over the tree roots so the tree appears to be on a hummock. Neither method is 100 per cent sure of keeping the tree in perfect health. But the chances of its living are much better. Small, young trees can be dug out and replanted at a lower or higher level as necessary.

5-3. Color In the Garden

By color in the garden, of course, we usually mean colors other than green, for that is the foliage and lawn color, and the background against which our other plants can show off their flowers. Fortunately we do not have to worry about color schemes, for there seems to be no clash among the colors of nature. Blues blend as well with green leaves as they do with red and orange flowers of other plants.

The gardener's usual aim is to have something in flower throughout the growing season. And plantsmen have made it easy for us. Modern annual flowers repeat their bloom through to frost even if we don't pick off all the old flower heads. Thus annuals provide us with our summer mainstay of color, preceded by the spring-flowering bulbs, spotlighted by herbaceous perennials and followed by chrysanthemums in fall. Even in tiny gardens, on apartment balconies, or in shady gardens that

Chrysanthemums are easy plants to move, even when they are in full flower.

get only a spot of sun, annuals can be grown in containers, moved to catch the sun or for best display. These can be discarded in early fall and replaced with 'mums in flower you've grown yourself in another part of the garden, or bought from a nurseryman. 'Mums are easy plants and can be moved even in full flower.

All leaves aren't green, however, and not all the color in the garden need come from flowers. Some plants, such as canna lilies with their spotted red, green or bronzy leaves, offer leaf color as well as flower color. There is a variegated (mixed color) hosta or plantain lily for shady gardens. Dark Opal basil has red-purple leaves all season and makes a fine low hedge for the vegetable garden as well as supplying an herb for the table.

The old favorite house plant, coleus, offers different leaf textures and colors from jade green and chocolate brown through reds and yellows, often with as many as three or four colors in one leaf. Dusty miller and artemisia

Hot-colored trees such as flowering crabapples are ideal accent plants, especially for a city garden.

provide silver. Caladiums in humusy soil and with good moisture supply will produce huge leaves of many colors throughout the season: silver and green, red and white, red, green and white.

Some shrubs offer mixed colored leaves. Silver-leafed dogwood is green and white. So is evergreen Emerald Gaiety euonymus. There are golden privets, golden mock oranges, golden junipers and cedars, and blue-leafed evergreens — Colorado blue spruce and Blue Haven juniper are best-sellers for just that reason.

Lately, plants with red, maroon and purple foliage have gained a vogue, spiked by the success of Crimson King and Royal Red maples, produced by grafts from Schwedler's Norway maple, a variety that comes out in maroon-red leaves in spring. (These later turned green but one plant produced a branch whose leaves kept their red color all season and all Crimson Kings have been produced from that.)

There are red-leafed and purple-leafed Japanese maples, purple-leafed plum, Royalty flowering crabapple, purple sand cherry, and Shubert's purple chokecherry (which starts out with green leaves that later turn purple-red). There are bronze-leafed and purple-leafed birch and beech trees. Though generally less vigorous than their green-leafed counterparts, such hot-colored trees can certainly spice up the garden. They are ideal accent plants, especially for the city garden of the cottage commuter who can't look after an ordinary flower garden over the summer. They are invaluable in providing summer color to a low maintenance garden composed almost entirely of shrubs, trees and grass, where the flowering shrubs brighten spring, with perhaps only a hydrangea and summer spirea or tamarisk to bloom in summer. In a combined planting that includes plants with bright fall leaf color, they bridge the gap. And that is the way they should be used — as accent plants. The danger in using too many of them, or in planting only red-leafed shrubs and trees, is that they look hot in the dog days of summer when the last thing you need is a hot color, and when undiluted green is most attractive.

Nor do red-leafed plants such as these maintain color in fall. Their leaves merely turn brown and drop.

5-4. Color In Fall and Winter

It's obvious we look to our gardens for color or why else would we plant all those flowers? But what about those other times of the year when the flowers don't bloom? Is the garden to be a dead thing during the greater portion of the year in a cold climate? It needn't be. Although there is no way we can duplicate the brilliant colors of late spring and summer, there are ways of adding color — and interest — over virtually 12 months of the year. With a little careful planning, using trees and shrubs with several seasons' interest, it should be possible to have color in your garden all year.

Assuming that summer annual flowers, summer bulbs and perennials brighten the garden from late spring to Labor Day or later, the tendency is to feel the garden is gone for another year when the first killing frost hits. The tree leaves fall, and in most areas there is very little to interest the eye outdoors until the snow falls. Even then we tend to think of the landscape as frozen and uninteresting.

And what about that dullest of times, early spring after the snow melts but before the grass turns green, when everything has a gray cast even on a bright sunny day?

Start with fall. Have at least one tree or shrub with bright fall leaf color. Most native maples offer fall leaf color in the red-orange range. There are compact versions of the sugar and native red maples available for the small properties. The Amur river maple colors brightly if briefly, is very hardy and will fit into almost any small property.

The red and pin oaks offer scarlet and purple. Mountain ash and flowering cherry turn dull scarlet. Some flowering crabapples and dawn redwood turn bronze before they drop their leaves.

One of the most brilliant red colors of all is provided by the winged euonymus or spindle

Winter aconite, the earliest-blooming flower, will appear in March in a protected spot. (Photo by Malak)

tree (which is also called "burning bush"); sumac leaves, while coarse, turn a brilliant scarlet. Azaleas and high bush blueberries are almost worth planting for fall color alone, and Boston ivy and its relative, Virginia creeper, have good color. Birches, poplar and larches turn yellow before their leaves drop.

The garden begins to look bare when those colored leaves finally drift down. But still there are plants with color. Many evergreens put on a purplish color for winter, including some low junipers and Oregon grape holly. And still others have colorful fruit. Hawthorns and bush roses sport bright red hips. Yews have bright red berries (to say nothing of holly berries where holly is hardy) and junipers have blue ones to contrast with their foliage. Euonymus and firethorn have orange-red fruit. Mountain ash fruit varies from coral to fiery red and tends to hang on well into winter when it is not eaten by birds (reason enough to plant one). Viburnums of one kind or another have bright coral to red fruit. (The native high bush cranberry's fruit makes delicious jelly.)

As the season progresses there are fewer and fewer sources of color in the gardens. Most of the tall evergreens take on a sombre green color. It is then that the Colorado blue spruce (and its named varieties) are even more valuable in the landscape — last season's growth is still a bright blue color. And even if you can't afford the space for a full-size tree, there are dwarf or ball-shaped ones that won't grow three feet high in 15 years, but have the same bluish color on the new growth.

Cherry tree bark has a dull red flecked pattern with a warm glow in the winter sun. And the white bark of paper birch is never more attractive than when poking through the snow when the light is bluish and the shadows long in midwinter. The native red maple's twigs are a bright red, as are the stems of the red osier dogwood, while the grape holly maintains its bronzy-purple color to leaves above the snowline if the weather is not too severe.

Shortly after the snow goes, when things look grayest, we depend on some new green appearing in our lawns. As this happens (and sometimes before), the native red maples open minute red flowers to start the season off. Then come the crocuses and little spring bulbs to tide us over till the bigger bulbs and flowering shrubs start the season of growth again.

5-5. Water In the Garden

The sound and look of water have always fascinated mankind and many home gardeners want to incorporate it into their landscape. Unless you live beside an ocean, lake or watercourse, however, it presents special problems.

If the water is not running, provision must be made to keep it sweet and prevent it becoming stagnant and smelly. On small pools and fish ponds a suction pump may be the simple answer. Simply replace the water once a week over the season. Provide for a cover over winter so there is no hazard.

A very simple reflecting or fish pool can easily be constructed in a day using a modest excavation, black plastic sheet, natural rocks

Many home gardeners incorporate water into their landscapes; here, a pool corner is planted with arrowhead.

Gardening by a stream, river or lake should be restrained so that full use is made of the view.

and a little mortar to hold the rocks together. Fold the edges of the plastic under so that the rocks, arranged around the outer lip, hide it. Apply the mortar and let it harden before filling the pool. If the excavation is at least a foot deep you won't have to change the water so often.

More permanent pools can be made with poured concrete. But to be relatively safe from frost action the footings should go below the frost line and this makes the project a big one (the frost may break apart the mortared rocks on the plastic-lined pool, but that is a simple matter to fix the next year, when it is a good idea to replace the plastic anyway.

Pools look more natural if there is a background such as a log, some evergreens, a fern or two. They do not look natural in the center of a grassy area with no other plants around. And in such a location they become a walking hazard, especially at night.

Kits are available with pools and spouting or drip fountains powered by a circulating pump so the same water is used over and over. Other kits will claim to provide you with a waterfall that emulates nature. Beware of the plastic ones that never do quite look like rock. On the other hand there are kinds with a lightweight rock that can be arranged to look as natural as the real thing. Again, try to arrange the planting so the waterfall and the plants look as though they belong together.

Gardening by a real stream or lake should be restrained so that you make use of the view. In many cases all that is required is to remove the underbrush and lower branches, and cut the grass so that you can walk or sit and take in the waterscape. Dug-out pools look best if grassed to a sand beach area, with perhaps some large stones arranged to look as though they happened naturally.

Elements of Landscaping: Garden Goofs, or What to Avoid

As discussed, North American gardening is aimed at pleasing the gardener as well as making an attractive property that everyone can appreciate. There are not so many rules or restrictions as there would be if you were trying to produce a French, Italian or Spanish garden, where straight lines, precise measurements and rather limited color contrasts of plant material are absolute requirements. In other words, we are casual in our gardens. We can afford to mix formal and informal plants, low and high, colored foliage with green, annuals, bulbs, ground covers, needle-leafed and broad-leafed evergreen shrubs, flowers of every color. Nevertheless there are some simple directives that can help you make better use of your property, and that will improve its looks to you as well as to everybody else.

People who love plants but have no clear plan of what a garden should look like are an example of the gardener who uses his property unwisely. They bring home plants they like or bargains they don't want to pass by. Then comes the job of getting them into the ground. A hole must be dug somewhere — anywhere. After a number of years the space at the back or front is pocked with planting holes and there are the plants, an obstacle course for the mower or even for the gardener trying to cross the yard.

This kind of garden just grows and grows until it suddenly becomes a kind of jungle. It's not inviting to use, to look at or to maintain. Eventually, of course, someone — perhaps a subsequent owner — has to start chopping down and starting over again.

We call this "booby-trap planting". So heedless of the final result, this stuffing of plants into any old place that is vacant ignores the need for sitting area, sunning area, service and play areas.

Single shrubs, evergreens, rosebushes, clumps of perennials or spring-flowering bulbs planted singly or even in small clumps without relation to each other or to an overall plan achieve only a cluttered look. Similarly, a line of single plants, say tulips or petunias, has a ragged appearance and never achieves a splash or even a spot of color that the same number of plants would have if grouped together. And the grouping takes far less work in cultivating, weeding and watering than the strung-out line.

Trees and shrubs planted this way provide neither privacy nor good looks. For example, a single flowering shrub in a lawn can be your garden's spectacular display. So may a single evergreen. Or, lined up along the edge of the property, they could screen you from the street or from neighbors. Planted to one side of a high building, they can tie it into the ground and make it look mellower.

Evergreen and deciduous shrubs in a small grouping are, like the flowers mentioned above, much easier to maintain. They also offer a focal point to the eye while freeing the rest of the garden space for other uses.

There certainly are times for massed plantings. On a large property a combination of evergreens, deciduous trees and lower shrubs planted in front can give the effect of a small wood. It could effectively block out an unwanted sight, such as a parking lot or a commercial area, and it helps to absorb noise and air pollution from the street. But again, this is an organized planting with a special purpose in mind. You don't necessarily have to have a graph paper plan, although some people find this a good way to plan their garden. But if it isn't down on paper, you do need to have a picture in your mind of how the garden is going to look when it is finished.

6-1. Avoid Cliché Plantings

There may be times when setting a shade tree dead center in a lawn enhances the garden, but it is unlikely. Yet this garden cliché is repeated time after time. Either the gardener doesn't think ahead and just takes the easiest way out when it comes time to set a tree in the ground, or he or she is a mathematician at heart. But a mathematical approach to what should, after all, be a natural-appearing garden winds up instead with an angular appearance that pleases no one. Centered on a lawn, usually of small size, the tree effectively dominates it so that the lawn appears much smaller than it really is. If the tree is allowed to keep all its lower branches, there is no room to sit under it and enjoy its shade.

This bull's-eye type of planting focuses attention on two objects, the tree itself and the house separately, whereas if the tree were planted to either side and nearer the house it would complement the lines of the house and free the front lawn.

A determined bull's-eye planter will compound the cliché by cultivating all around the tree and planting rings of petunias or pansies,

or both. This quickly achieves a roadside hotdog stand appearance, wastes more usable space and requires a great deal more maintenance.

Consider the alternative, even if you want a tree dead center. Grow grass right up to the trunk the way trees are grown in most parks. Mowing is far easier than planting and taking care of annual flowers, which also requires constant edging of the grass. Clipping the grass beside the trunk need only be done every second or third mowing. The area under the tree's branch spread then becomes available for other purposes such as sitting or playing. And the bull's-eye effect is reduced. The green background shows off the tree to better advantage. The only precaution is to avoid bashing the bark by trying to get too close with the power mower.

If one tree centered on a lawn cuts down considerably on usable lawn space, consider the ultimate in mathematical gardening: a centered paved walk and two trees, each centered on the half lawn to each side of the sidewalk. The static balance of this scene dulls the senses and makes the garden look like one of those papier-mâché models that supposedly represents a garden. You could save half the work and gain twice the effect by planting a tree on one side only. But choose the south or west side so you can get the most benefit from the shade in the heat of the afternoon.

6-2. Straight Line Clichés

Unfortunately most building lots are laid out by surveyors and engineers, not by gardeners. The result, as we all know, is that they are for the most part rectangular. This rectangle is usually long and narrow, so the gardener is extremely limited by what he has to start with. Unfortunately the cliché gardener will compound the problem by stringing a hedge or a mixed shrub planting down the property line from top to bottom. This cuts down on the width and adds to the angular look, whereas

Planting flowers around the base of a tree is not always advisable, especially if the tree is planted in the center of a lawn.

scalloped, clump or oval planting areas with their curved lines would give the illusion of a spacious garden with points of interest here and there.

Even if a straight line planting seems more practical to you, try to get that curved look by planting shrubs of varying shapes and heights and let them grow to their natural shape without pruning. Hedges have uses, as we've seen, but on a long narrow lot they overemphasize the linear. Instead, consider other ways to lay out your yard. You could, for example, base it on an oval with one pointed end where your sitting area or patio is, and the other diagonally opposite. This would give an illusion of greater depth to a short yard with your eye travelling to the far end. There you could have a fountain, a garden seat around a shade tree, a specimen plant — perhaps a spectacular flowering shrub — or a rose garden. Perhaps even a bed of annuals would do the trick.

Other possibilities include pocket or mini-gardens either in a continuous or scalloped garden, or in separate pockets or scallops along the fence line; low hedges, perhaps of Korean boxwood or arctic willow, to mark off a reflecting pool, an herb or rose garden, a kitchen garden of salad fixings or a cutting garden where you grow flowers like and with vegetables, not for their landscape effect but to provide continuous bouquets for the table.

The possibilities for arranging your grounds into interesting and useful gardening areas are limited only by your imagination and the actual dimensions of the space you're working with. There is no reason why you should be satisfied with or limited to that rectangle the subdivider left you with.

There are other garden clichés, too, that seem obvious to all but the owner, but if he or she is satisfied, that matters most. However, he or she might like gardening even more if they could see an improvement in looks of house and grounds. Many gardeners rely on a gimmick (everyone has seen wagon wheel plantings) and will latch onto almost anything to try to improve nature. We have seen old buggies, wheelbarrows, old bathtubs, and even a toilet bowl full of bright petunias, apparently offered as the show garden in front of a modest bungalow.

Not quite so bad but still out of proportion is a bed of flamboyant canna lilies in front of a modest bungalow on a small lot. Beds of cannas are colorful — and suitable — in a public park or on a large estate. By a small house they look gross.

6-3. Know How Big It Will Grow

It is hard to bear in mind the eventual size of a tree or shrub when you have a lot of space to landscape and you're buying small sizes. That baby Colorado blue spruce looks so cute there is a tendency to plant it close to a house window or right beside the path or the driveway. At first it grows slowly and causes no trouble. But soon it is putting on eight to 10 inches of height each year and a foot or more in girth. It shuts light from the window summer and winter (when you need it most) or its branches overlap the sidewalk or driveway. Of course there is no alternative at this point but to cut it down, or to remove the offending branches, rendering the tree lopsided.

Similarly it may always have been your dream to have a sugar maple on your property. But sugar maples, like other forest trees, seldom have a place on small city lots. The trees themselves suffer, with their roots crammed into small spaces between paved areas and where their branches are likely to be pruned to benefit utility wires, not the shape and health of the tree. The time to think of this is before you choose your tree.

Check eventual heights and spreads with a local nurseryman or in a good nursery catalogue. Also check whether roots may damage sewer pipes. After 15 years a delightful weeping willow on our neighbor's lot had to be removed, leaving the front of his house as bare as it was when he bought it new from the builder. The willow's roots had got into the sewer pipe and cost him $300 for sewer repairs plus the cost of removing the willow.

Poplar trees are tempting to new home owners, or to those who have just lost an old

A mature eastern white pine may reach a height of 80 feet; they are too big for all but the largest properties.

A dwarf mugho pine hedge must be clipped regularly or it will reach heights of six feet, too tall for most home gardens.

tree, since they grow so fast. However, they too can damage sewer lines, swimming pools and other conduits. They may even damage the basement walls of houses up to 40 feet away, to say nothing of rendering the ground all around useless for any other gardening purpose.

The same principle, on a smaller scale, applies to so-called dwarf evergreens. Two common plants used in foundation plantings are Pfitzer juniper and mugho pine. Yet if unpruned, as they are in most home gardens, both will eventually grow as tall as an adult person and six feet across. So either buy smaller plants, or allow them enough room.

The latter course will leave great gaps in an evergreen planting, if you start with young plants. But you can always fix that by using spring-flowering bulbs planted in fall, summer annual flowers planted in spring, tuberous begonias and chrysanthemums for fall bloom.

Gardens are not static. As the small evergreens gain maturity, you'll need less and less material to fill in between, until finally they grow together. At this point you can decide whether to remove some, do considerable pruning, or just enjoy the full look of such a mature planting.

6-4. Annuals and Vegetables Need Room Too

Many gardeners suffer from the same urge to fill the available space in their annual flower, perennial, rose or vegetable gardens. If they do, however, they are rewarded with a jungle, not the garden they thought they were going to get. Each plant needs space to develop and produce properly, whether a flower or a vegetable. That's the whole point — the difference between the way plants look in gardens and the way they look in the natural state when left to compete for space, light and water. In fact, more home vegetable gardens fail for lack of thinning than for any other single factor. It doesn't matter to a radish whether its competition is a dandelion or another radish, if it can't get what it needs when it needs it.

Cultivated, bare ground between plants doesn't necessarily appear ugly, but if it bothers you cover it with a loose, light material that looks attractive. Some examples are chunky peat moss, wood chips, bark chips, cocoa bean hulls (which, however, have a tendency to blow away), partly rotted leaf mould, dried grass clippings, half-rotted sawdust. Another approach would be to set shrubs, or evergreens, say, in individual planting holes, but with an integrated planting plan in mind. Grass would provide the ground covering between young plants.

As the plants grow larger, enlarge the cultivated area around them until finally they merge and the integrated planting is clear. Alternatively you could prepare the whole area, plant the young shrubs suitably far apart and use a vine or other ground cover to bridge the gaps between the young plants.

6-5. Avoid One-Season Gardens

There's a very great tendency when we see, say, spring-flowering shrubs in bloom, to want to fill the yard with them. Of course they are beautiful and in the spring there is nothing to compare with Japanese cherries, flowering crabs or almonds. A month later, there's nothing to compare with lilacs. Similarly, the gardener who loves iris, delphinium, peonies or any other flowering plant, is tempted to make a whole garden of his favorite. Unfortunately that results in a one-season garden that peaks and then loses interest. While still green for the rest of the summer, it literally lacks color and may have no winter interest at all.

In effect the specialty becomes a cliché in your garden. But by tempering your passions and planning ahead for other seasons, you can include shrubs that bloom in summer, say; trees and shrubs with brilliant fall color, evergreens with interesting foliage color or texture for fall and winter interest, and spring-flowering bulbs (that must be planted in fall) for color between the time the snow leaves and the first shrubs bloom.

While it's not always possible to have a genuine four-seasons garden in northern climates, there is no reason why with planning and forethought you cannot have some interesting landscapes outside your picture window all year long.

Just a note of caution, though, on choosing too many plants with arresting interest. Trees and shrubs with red or purple leaves have become very popular lately. Crimson King maple, purple-leaf plum, purple sandcherry and purple chokecherry, purple and bronze-leafed beech are valuable accent plants. But planted alone or with other red-leafed plants, they dominate the landscape with a hot color, far from relaxing on a steamy summer day. Use them as contrast against a background of green so they provide color interest without taking it over.

Having said all this about choosing plants for all-season interest, there still should be room for special plants with a brief but spectacular season. We have a "tree" peony shrub that we wouldn't part with for the world, although it is undistinguished all summer and has an ugly, bare stick appearance after the leaves fall. But the brief, spectacular show of its giant purple flowers with yellow stamens two weeks ahead of ordinary herbaceous peonies entitles it to space in our small city garden.

Similarly, we give space to a Saskatoon serviceberry bush because of its prolific production of delicious fruit, although many other shrubs have more decorative leaves, twig formation or flowers.

6-6. Tell Others What You're Doing

It's a good idea to let your family know what you are doing in the garden, even if it means you pin up a plan or a chore sheet in the garage or shed and tick off or write down not only what you are doing now, but what needs to be done. This simple procedure can help you avoid a lot of garden goofs. If one gardener likes roses and the other likes vegetables, it makes sense to divide up the yard, hopefully within an overall plan, rather than try to grow both together, or to squabble over whose plants are usurping space from the others.

The garden bulletin board is a good idea even if there is only one gardener in the family. We can remember many a time slicing through tulip bulbs forgotten in the fall when transplanting a shrub. There was not only the actual loss of the bulbs, but all the effort that went into planting them. By that time it was too late to buy new bulbs and replant, so we lost a whole year through carelessness.

6-7. Cutting Corners Makes More Work

Similarly, gardeners may cut corners when planting. This may range from lack of soil preparation to omitting to drive a stake. Lack of soil preparation, particularly under lawns, can only mean much heavier maintenance in years to come. Omitting the stake at planting time can result in spoiled plants. If you drive the stake later, you may drive it right through the plant's root system. If you don't use a stake at all, the plant may grow crooked and be damaged by storms, or, in the case of a sapling tree, may be completely uprooted by a strong wind following a heavy rainstorm.

Cutting corners always seems the easiest way out, particularly if you have other things pressing, or if you are out planting on a miserable, wet day. It's cheaper, simpler and infinitely easier to dig a small hole and stuff the plant's roots in, tromping the old soil back on top. But you pay in poor growth and sickly plants over the years to come, if indeed the plant survives the first season. Follow the planting instructions in the other volume on gardening in this series, entitled *Sowing and Growing a Garden*.

Similarly with tulips, it's much easier to use a bulb-planting tool to excavate a few inches of soil, pop a bulb in, and replace the soil than it is to excavate a bed deeply, prepare the soil under where the bulbs will sit (that's where their roots feed), place the bulbs carefully and then fill prepared earth back. But proper preparation can produce good tulip flowers for up to 10 years from the same planting while the maximum from short-cut planting may be only three.

6-8. Fixing Goofs That Aren't Your Fault

Sometimes you'll discover, long after the planting season is over, that there's a bare or brown patch on the lawn, that a key perennial, shrub evergreen or rosebush hasn't survived the winter. Perhaps you were even suspicious of it the year before, but waited to see if it would come back. Probably the bitterest disappointment is when a newly-planted shade tree fails to leaf out. You've been waiting for those first signs of growth and told yourself it was just late. Now it seems there's no hope and you're going to have to wait a year to plant another.

Few gardeners indeed carry spare plants in out-of-the-way corners of the garden for just such an emergency. There are, however, some remedies at hand. Some are permanent cures for garden gaposis; others will provide only temporary cures, but will fill the gap for one season.

One of the easiest cures is to inspect the container-grown plants at your local nurseries. Many nurserymen grow a great number of plants in pots, from fruit trees to perennials, including evergreens, shade trees and roses. If you are careful in planting you can in effect defy the season and set out a shade tree in July, if it is necessary to replace a dead one.

If, for example, there's a gap or two in the rose garden from plants that started to leaf out in spring and then suddenly gave up the effort and died, you may be able to buy rose plants, some in full bloom, growing in containers. Those in fiber pots can be planted pot and all in a prepared hole. The sides of the pot should be scored and no part of the pot should show above the soil line.

In a similar way you can replace a dead shade tree with one from a nursery that has been grown in a bushel basket, with no disturbance to its roots. In either case, the basket or the fiber eventually will disintegrate in the soil. Of course, watering is critical and it may be wise to wrap the trunk of the tree with kraft paper to prevent sunscald.

If the replacement plant is growing in a clay pot or metal can, it must be removed before planting. This is a little trickier. Water first, then run a long knife along the inside of the container. Holding the pot between your feet, grasp the stem and pull evenly until the rootball comes away. Set it directly in a prepared hole with the minimum exposure to sun and air. It is essential that you do not break the rootball and lose the soil around the roots.

As discussed in detail in the other volume on gardening in this series, water all new transplants with a high phosphorus transplanter solution (grade 10:52:17 or 10:45:15) to lessen root shock. At subsequent waterings, wet down the foliage especially on hot days to help reduce the chances of wilting.

Don't ignore the obvious remedies of boxed annual plants and potted geraniums. Many nurseries and stores that sell boxed annual flowers have stock left over from the big spring sale rush, some even as late as August. It's true the plants look rather bedraggled: they certainly aren't first quality at this date. But planted with care and watered faithfully, they will come on quickly with a rush of color. And as for geraniums, these great old reliables are available as pot plants the year round. They've fixed more holes in gardens and planter boxes than any other single plant, substituting for dead perennial, rose, bulb, shrub and even evergreen, and will bloom from planting till killing frost or until you make a permanent replacement.

6-9. Replacement Sources In Your Own Garden

Your own garden may be the source of the replacements you need. Most home gardeners plant too close together, anyway, and it will often improve an annual flower garden to remove several if not many plants, allowing the rest to reach proper development. These can be moved after sunset, preferably just before a cloudy or rainy day, if you dig up a good-sized clump of soil that remains unbroken around the roots. Such spare plants can be used to thicken out another place where seed germination was poor and the flowers scattered, or as summer replacements for more permanent plants that have failed. (Some gardeners deliberately plant extra annuals in an out-of-the-way spot each spring for just such a purpose, and to have fresh plants to replace bedraggled ones in midsummer.)

Some perennials can be divided even if it is not the ideal season to do so. A large iris rhizome (fleshy rootstalk) with several fans of leaves can be dug, divided and replanted from spring to fall (although the proper season is after flowers have faded in July). Each division with two or more sets of leaves will make a mature plant within a year, and can certainly substitute for a victim of the fatal iris borer.

Some other perennials will lend themselves to the same treatment. Examples are delphinium, chrysanthemums, hibiscus and other multi-stemmed plants that either have many stems from a crown that can be divided, or that have tuberous, spreading roots which support many top shoots.

Division in midseason will work with shrubs such as barberry, euonymus, juniper, yew, chamaecyparis. The method is often referred to as a "Dutch cutting". Essentially it consists in separating a piece of hard root with many feeder (hair) roots intact, that also has some top growth with foliage. Other ready-made plants occur where a lower branch has been touching moist earth for some years, and roots have formed at the point of contact. Such volunteer replacement plants can be found on Eastern white cedar (arborvitae), juniper, lilac, forsythia and others.

6-10. Quick Lawn Cures

While permanent bluegrasses in our lawns do creep by underground rootstalk and will eventually heal dead areas, it sometimes takes too long and allows weeds to gain a foothold. Today it is easy enough to buy as little as one roll of sod from which you can cut patches to fit your needs. But there is a source of replacement grass in your own yard. Every time you edge around a walk, hedge, garden or tree, you cut out (and probably discard) grass plants complete with roots and soil. These can easily be salvaged and either pieced together in a dead area, or used separately as plugs set into thin lawn areas. Unwanted grass plants that have volunteered in flower and shrub gardens can be used the same way. Going one step further, you could maintain a tiny sod nursery in a section of the vegetable garden as an instant source of patching sod for the lawn. It goes without saying that all such repairs need careful attention to watering if they are to take and grow vigorously.

You can produce a temporary lawn in 10 days to two weeks on any area that you want covered but couldn't get seeded with permanent grass at the proper time. Perennial ryegrass is a tough, coarse, vigorous grass that sprouts within days in warm, moist weather, and becomes established in two weeks. Plow it under when you're ready to seed with good permanent grass.

Seed or Sod?

A good green lawn front and back to show off our houses and other garden plants is essential to North American home landscaping. This is probably directly derived from English gardening where rich greenswards are the rule. Unfortunately the climate in most areas of North America is not usually so conducive to growing grass as easily as in England, and we have to do a little work to achieve a green effect from spring thaw to winter freeze-up. Few gardeners would dispute the effort is worth it, even if the weather often seems determined to oppose us.

If you're starting from bare soil, or turning under an old lawn for a fresh start, you'll have to decide whether to grow your own grass from seed, buy sod or have a contractor take over the job.

You can grow equally good lawns from seed or sod — the essential thing is to prepare the soil well ahead of time. Seed is considerably cheaper but grass plants take up to two years to mature and form a thick-knit ground cover. Sod, as the sod suppliers are fond of reporting, will produce an almost instant lawn.

There are only two times of the year to sow grass seed with hope of good results fairly quickly and without reseeding, as we shall see later. On the other hand, sod can be laid whenever you can get it from the supplier up to about a month before freeze-up, although spring and late summer are still best.

There are problems in getting sod to take and to stay green during hot, dry summer weather that favors grass dormancy. And you can get hung up with a delivery of sod during a rainy spell. Left in rolls the sod may grow into itself so the rolls become impossible to separate. Of course you can avoid this problem by hiring a contracting firm to do the soil preparation and laying, making sure you get a guarantee that the sod will take, or they'll come back to fix it.

7-1. Make Sure They Do It Right

If you do hire the work out, make sure you get them to prepare the soil properly, before you let them unfurl one roll.

Good lawns that require low maintenance are possible only when there is good under-drainage, and a minimum of six inches of topsoil, or of a mixture of subsoil and humus (plus sand in clays). The mixture should resemble the ideal soil described in Chapter 3.

When grass is cut at a height of two inches, probably the best height for the average home lawn, the roots will penetrate the soil to about six inches. If this soil is easily permeated by air and water the grass plants will be healthy and vigorous.

Mechanical applicators apply seed and fertilizer quickly, accurately and economically.

7-2. Fertilizer for Good Roots

If you are amending the soil you have, be sure to add some chemical fertilizer before you mix humus and subsoil together. Various ratios are promoted for lawn building, but you can use any kind with high middle and last figures. Examples are 4:12:10, 5:10:15 (for sands) and 10:20:10. The point is to try to encourage strong root growth rather than rapid production of green leaves. Ordinary lawn fertilizers such as 20:10:5 are designed to do the opposite on established lawns. The amount to use is determined by the first figure of the ratio. Divide it into 100 and use the result in pounds on each 1,000 square feet, along with the humus and sand if necessary. A rotary tiller makes the job easier.

If your garden soil is already good and you decide you don't need any additives, don't forget the land must be graded before seeding and sodding. Scrape the topsoil off into a pile to one side. Then grade the subsoil so that the surface drainage will be away from buildings to a storm sewer, ditch or city street. Paths should stand just slightly higher than the grass; otherwise they will act as a drain. In winter this may mean a sheet of ice to walk on most of the time.

7-3. Watch Eavestrough Water

At this time it is also wise to make arrangements for disposal of water from eavestroughs, if they are not connected directly to a storm sewer. Red weeping tile laid under the ground will carry off the water without washing out soil. There are roll-out perforated bags that can be attached to down pipes that let the water out gradually with benefit to the lawn. Even simpler is to let the downspouts splash out on a small piece of plywood or on a piece of rock.

7-4. Special Treatment for Slopes

While grass can be grown on steep slopes, it is difficult not only to get it established, but also to keep it mowed. There are several ways of handling slopes. If it is not to stand foot traffic, one of a number of ground covers may do the trick. But the simplest way of all is to create a lawn at different levels by using a retaining wall. Such a wall may be made of dry masonry, such as cement blocks, flagstones or bricks, set progressively back into the hill, with earth fill tamped in place as the masonry units are added. Vertical cedar poles are attractive, or the poles could be fitted length-wise and held in place with other poles or steel stakes driven into the ground. (Steel stakes may also be used this way through the centers of hollow concrete blocks to make a dry wall more rigid.)

Cemented or mortared masonry walls are more attractive to some people, but they won't last the first winter in most northern regions unless there are adequate footings — usually poured concrete — that go below the frost line. Cemented retaining walls have the added advantage of being virtually weed-free, at least at first, while dry walls and log retainers do tend to have weeds growing in the joints.

7-5. Spread Topsoil Evenly

Once the land grading has been completed,

spread the topsoil you've saved in a pile evenly over the whole lawn area.

Is it worth buying topsoil? It may be if your pocketbook can stand it and if you get an ironclad guarantee that it is sterilized or at least has no pieces of couch grass roots in it. Couch grass is one of the worst garden pests. Going by a number of names (including twitch or quack grass), it has to be grubbed out by hand, since any weedkiller that will kill it will also kill good grasses.

Home gardeners frequently ask if it is possible to improve the soil under lawns by top-dressing with any one of a number of products from topsoil to peat moss. The latter is of very different texture and should be mixed with the soil first, not added in layers afterward. And topsoil, while it can be raked over lawns in thin applications of 1/4 to 1/2 inch at a time, takes forever to build up an appreciable amount under the sod. The only time it's really worthwhile is if you are trying to keep grass growing on top of surface-rooting trees such as poplars and maples.

Grass will do the job just about as quickly itself if you water as needed, if you maintain a good fertilizing schedule and if you cut frequently so the clippings are short and can remain where they fall, and rot down to create a humusy topsoil. In addition to these factors, grass has the habit of sloughing off some of its old roots. These decay, forming tiny veins of humus in the soil. Of course these things take a lot of time to form any appreciable amount of topsoil.

While good care can increase the rate of decay, it is still going to take heavy mainte-nance for many, many years unless you start with real or manufactured topsoil. And at first you'll be fighting what seems a losing battle against foot traffic, weeds and hot summer weather, for shallow-rooted grasses have little or no resistance.

7-6. Advantages of Grass Seed

Besides the economy of growing grass from seed, this method of making a lawn also gives

Seed or Sod? 75

you a wide choice of grass varieties. Sod growers must standardize their operations to one or two kinds and sometimes you can't get the mixture you want. Obviously if you are buying seed you can mix or sow whatever pure strains of permanent lawn grasses you wish, alone or in a mixture.

New varieties such as Fylking, Nugget and Barron bluegrasses offer some better characteristics than plain Kentucky bluegrass. Nugget, for example, is dwarf and slow-growing so that it requires less cutting. It was found in Alaska and thus has great cold resistance. The others offer vigor and relative resistance to diseases, and very thick turf when watered and fertilized adequately.

Creeping red and Chewings fescue grasses are often used in mixtures with bluegrasses to provide a lawn that stands up to varying conditions. For one thing they tolerate more shade, and as your garden plants mature and the trees grow, the fescues can spread.

Also, in some seasons, weather and soil moisture conditions will favor bluegrasses over fescues or vice versa. A home lawn containing both kinds offers a sort of insurance. Fescues require less fertilization and less soil moisture than bluegrasses.

There are some other kinds of grasses you may want to consider. Canada bluegrass, for example, is a tough, coarse grass that will tolerate a variety of difficult conditions ranging from heavy clays to sands to wet areas. While it makes a coarse, open sod that would never become a fine lawn, it will withstand heavy foot traffic and bound back. Mixed in equal parts by weight with plain Kentucky bluegrass and creeping red fescue, Canada bluegrass will hold down sands and cover clay fields. Its fertilizer requirements are minimal, and once established it will get along well without irrigation. An even plainer mixture would be equal parts of Canada bluegrass and creeping red fescue.

7-7. Fast, Temporary Lawns

Common so-called "perennial" ryegrass is not perennial and not a useful grass in lawns, although it is sometimes added to commercial mixtures as a "nurse" grass. The idea is that because it germinates quickly it gives the gardener the feeling something is happening. (Kentucky bluegrasses may take up to four weeks to germinate in cold weather and many novice gardeners feel the seed has failed long before it could be expected to come up.) Germinating quickly, perennial ryegrass does provide some sort of shade for the slower bluegrasses and the intermediate fescues. But this soon turns to a disadvantage: the vigorous ryegrass seedlings take up the soil space and moisture, leaving little for the slower ones. Thus it's best to avoid ryegrass in lawn mixtures. Nevertheless, perennial ryegrass, which lasts about one or two seasons, is useful as a temporary lawn. Since it does germinate and grow quickly it can be used to provide a green cover on rough areas that you can't arrange to sod or seed with good grasses at the moment. It can be mowed, although it browns rather badly in midsummer. When you do plant permanent grasses the ryegrass can simply be tilled under where it helps add organic matter to the soil. (Perennial and annual ryegrass and even rye grain can be used to enrich the soil in this way in other than lawn areas; where it is not to be mowed it should be tilled into the soil after it reaches eight to 10 inches in height. You can repeat sowings over a season to gain several crops of "green manure", as it is sometimes called.)

There are two special selections of perennial ryegrass that are especially useful. Norlea, developed at Ottawa, has a deeper green color and more permanent nature, and can be used in mixtures, especially with Merion Kentucky Bluegrass; Manhattan perennial ryegrass also offers a deeper green color and more winter permanence. It establishes itself in as few as two weeks in suitable weather, making a walk-on surface about as fast as sodding. It is also valuable for fast repair of winter-killed patches, particularly on lawn areas that get heavy traffic and don't have to be manicured.

7-8. A Shade-Tolerant Grass

One other strain of grass that may help under special conditions is lesser bluegrass, sometimes called "rough-stalked meadowgrass". Botanically it is *poa trivialis.* Its color is an olive green compared to other bluegrasses and it has a glassy appearance. Nor will it stand up to foot traffic; and it tends to die out after two or three years. But it will grow in the dense shade between two buildings. So long as you can get a mower in, you might consider it if you have such a shady area. Otherwise, use some other kind of ground cover or pave such a tough area. *Poa trivialis* may be included with creeping red fescue for areas less densely shaded.

7-9. Clover is Not Grass

Clover is a legume and as such enriches the ground it is grown in through bacteria that form nodules on its roots which can fix atmospheric nitrogen. It is deep-rooted and thus can bring minerals up from subsoils and is able to withstand droughts. Only Dutch white variety of clover can withstand low mowing. It is so adaptable in a lawn it may drive out the grasses in patches. But then sometimes these patches winterkill, leaving large, bare areas. There are other disadvantages: lawn buffs object to the white flowers and the shape and color of the foliage which doesn't blend very well with grass. Also, the juice from the leaves will stain clothing and shoes. If the advantages outweigh the disadvantages for you, use about one quarter pound of Dutch white clover seed to 10 pounds of mixed grass seed.

Quantities of seed to use depend on the coarseness of the seed. Kentucky bluegrass has over 2,000,000 seeds to the pound, while ryegrass has under 300,000. Fescues lie somewhere between. It is not necessary to cover the ground with seed like a mulch.

Remember that every seed that germinates and lives will eventually produce a complete plant with several blades, and that good bluegrasses will creep underground and send up new shoots elsewhere.

Three pounds of fine-seeded grasses should cover an area of 1,000 square feet. Use around 10 pounds of coarse grasses. Mixtures would require an intermediate amount.

7-10. When to Seed

Unlike sod laying, grass should be seeded only at two periods of the season: early spring and late summer. Of these, late summer is the preferred time. The reasons are many. Late summer is the natural time when self-sown seed of wild grass plants germinate. The angle and color of the light from the sun favor root growth over top growth; so does the fact the nights are longer, and the dews begin to be heavy. The ground is warm, which speeds up germination, particularly of bluegrasses, and increases root vigor.

The next best time is in early spring as soon as the ground can be worked. Grass seed is hardy and can stand frosts, but germination then is slow. Don't expect good results if you let early spring slide by and try to seed a lawn in May, if a heat wave is likely to follow in your area.

It's a matter of mathematics determining how much sod you'll need and thus the ultimate cost. Sod is usually sold by the square yard and delivered in short rolls stacked one on top of another, grass side in. Price is given per square yard, but check out to find if that is delivered or pickup price. You may find quite a difference (it is almost never worth the cost to have small quantities delivered). Allow for wastage since you can never duplicate in a garden the calculations and pencil lines on paper.

Since soil preparation for seed or sod should be the same, a little calculation some evening will give you a clear picture of the difference in cost between the price of seed and sod for your lawn area. Then decide if having an instant lawn is worth the difference, bearing in mind that perennial lawn grasses take up to two years to mature and that you'll have to do some weed-killing along the way.

7-11. A Sod-Seed Compromise

Finally, you might want to consider a new product that serves to bridge the gap between seed and sod. It consists of grass seeds implanted in a slowly soluble material that you can roll out and peg on to the ground. The bluegrass seed has been soaked to dissolve out a natural germination inhibitor so that germination is very quick as soon as the material has been dampened down, and the grass plants become established that much sooner. Because the seed is precision-placed by machine ahead of time, it is much easier for the gardener to get an even "take" of grass plants than by hand sowing of loose seed. And it is certainly easier to get good germination on a slope. It is not foolproof, however. The seed must not dry out after being started or the tiny germinating seedlings will die. The rolls must be placed as carefully as sod, although they are a good deal lighter and easier to handle, and can be cut with scissors.

Grass grown from seed and sod will have good or bad results depending on the prior preparation of the soil and on the maintenance given after the lawns are established.

Seedlings, Saplings and Full-size Trees

The best source of new trees for your garden is likely to be the local nursery sales station, or that of a large grower who offers you a wide choice. Nursery-grown trees are uniform, have compact roots concentrated just under the trunk from years of root pruning, and are thus easier to transplant. You can inspect before buying and choose the one that suits you best. What you see is what you get. And you control the period of time between purchase and planting. If your sales station is within a few miles of your garden, that time may be a matter of minutes, adding greatly to the chances of successful transplanting.

Mail-order nurseries are a secondary source but may be the only way to obtain special varieties or special sizes, as noted below with respect to seedlings. They are also the most convenient in that you can order from a catalogue by mail and receive your package by mail or express without ever leaving your house. And if you don't live near a nursery sales station, mail-order houses can save you miles of travel.

Other sources are local stores, some nurseries included, that stock packaged plants. Be wary of these. There is nothing wrong with most such stock; some of it is very first quality. But what is wrong in many cases is the way the retailer takes care of it after it arrives. It is often stored in warehouses like so many balls of string and taken out when store space allows. This may or may not coincide with the best planting time. But what follows is worse. Stores are usually overheated to compensate for doors being opened frequently. As a result, temperatures are even higher than is comfortable for people, let alone plants.

Packaged plants are presumably dormant. To stay that way they should be kept very cool indeed. The result of hot, dry indoor temperatures is to force an unhealthy growth while the roots are still confined to a small space and to subject the plants to packing materials (usually peat or sawdust or a mixture) which are drying out. The plant quickly exhausts itself.

You can buy perfectly good plants (including roses) in packages in such stores, but make your purchase the day the merchandise comes into the store, and keep it outside in the cold till you can plant. In fact, the very same packaged plants are likely to be a lot better buy if the store itself keeps them outside, where the air is cool and moist, so long as there is shade from the sun.

8-1. Sizes Commonly Available

Nurseries sell trees in a number of sizes and with the roots packed in different ways. The commonest way of packing is what is called "bare-root". The plant may actually come in a package so the roots are not really bare to the air. But they are dug from the nursery rows bare before packaging. The packaging compresses the roots and some moisture-holding material is added to help keep them for a certain shelf-life.

Some new plastic packaging reportedly keeps plants fresh and in this case the roots really are bare. But the plastic can puncture too easily, or perhaps is not tied properly by the packers, resulting in dead and dying plants delivered in plastic.

Plants standing in soil or sawdust in nursery sales stations are also considered bare-rooted. These were dug from the growing area and placed under covering at the sales station for the buyers to look over. When you buy they are easily pulled out, roots intact, and then wrapped in burlap, kraft paper or plastic for you to take home.

Bare-root plants should either be planted at once, or heeled into the ground until they can be planted permanently. Heeling in consists of digging a shallow, angled trough in the ground deep enough to accommodate the roots, and preferably in a shady location. The angle should be such that the ground supports the tops while the trench takes the roots. Then throw damp soil over the roots until they are well covered. Keep it moist during the storage period. All bare-root plants should be set into their permanent locations before the new growth is apparent.

Plants that are particularly sensitive to moving or having their roots exposed to the air, such as evergreens of any size, magnolias, rhododendrons, plants in leaf and large trees, are often sold balled and burlapped (B and B). This means that they are dug from the nursery with a ball of soil around the roots. This soil is wrapped in burlap and tied to hold the soil intact.

B and B plants are relatively easy to transplant and there isn't quite the urgency to get them in the ground immediately as there is with bare-root plants. As long as the soil ball doesn't dry out, you can keep them on hand for several weeks. B and B plants are usually more expensive because of the extra labor involved and because of the extra weight in transporting them. (For an extra fee, some nurseries will ball and burlap seedlings or saplings if you wish.)

Plant growers are now often offering trees, shrubs and evergreens in containers. Such plants, genuinely grown in pots and not stuffed into them just prior to sale, offer certain advantages. Like B and B plants, they do not have to be planted immediately. Indeed, you can grow some hardy evergreens in their containers for several years. Container plants are easier to transport than B and B and they are slower to dry out. If the pot is made of fiber, you can set it into the ground as is, so that summer planting becomes feasible. Thus you can fill a hole in a planting at any time in the growing season, although best results come from planting during the traditional season. Container plants, like B and B, cost more than bare-root ones. Sizes vary from seedlings a few years old to what are called "mature specimens". The latter are usually large enough to provide some shade the same year they are planted.

8-2. Big Trees, Big Job

A five- to six-foot blue spruce, a notorious slow grower in its early years, may run close to $200, as may a 15- to 20-foot maple. In some cases trees of this size are sold by their height. But often they are described as so many inches caliper. This refers to the diameter of the stem or trunk 12 inches above ground level. This is a better measure of the age of the tree than height alone, but you should take both into account for any you buy. Generally, though, these large nursery specimens are too difficult for a home gardener to handle alone, unless he has power equipment at hand. While some large specimens can be moved bare-root in the dormant season, most should be moved with a ball of soil undisturbed around the roots, which adds extra cost, and a great deal of extra weight; hence the need for power equipment. In general it is better to hire this done from a landscape contractor, or from the nursery where you buy the tree. Shop around for the best guarantee, as well as the best price. And insist the work be done during the dormant season: early spring before any sign of new growth for both evergreens and deciduous trees; again at the end of August for a month or so for evergreens, and after the first killing frost or after the leaves turn color (whichever comes first) for deciduous trees. If the hole is prepared ahead of time, such a tree can be moved in midwinter if there is access.

8-3. Seedlings Are Cheapest

At the other extreme in size are seedlings. These may be from two to seven years old if evergreens, and from one to three or four years old if deciduous trees. Seedlings are quite cheap and may often be purchased in lots from 10 to 1,000. Thus they are within most budgets for reforesting, to control erosion, and to produce extensive windbreaks or hedges where the gardener would be straining his budget (to say the least) if he were to buy large specimens. In most cases these small sizes are available through specialty nurseries which will ship by express or arrange for personal pickup. Seedlings are invariably sold bare-rooted, packed in moist sphagnum moss or sawdust, and then packaged in plastic with the tops out so they can breathe. Several hundred seedling trees would fit in an overnight bag. These small plants should be treated as live and perishable. Get them into a moist, shady area of the garden as soon as they arrive, pending planting.

Seedling trees and even those grown from seed, if handled properly, are a perfectly good way in which you can afford a lot of trees on your property — if you are content to wait a long time for them to get big. Thus, buying seedlings suits young gardeners on a raw piece of land, or those starting early to prepare a retirement place in the country.

If you decide to buy seedlings, particularly if evergreens, choose the oldest ones offered.

The price difference may be considerable on large numbers, but it's not much per tree. One nursery may, for example, offer Douglas fir in two sizes: two-year seedlings between five and 10 inches tall at 100 for $8, and five-year transplants six to 10 inches tall at $20 per 100. That $12 difference seems a lot but the most expensive only cost 20 cents a tree. For the extra 12 cents the nursery has grown the plants three more years and has transplanted them once from the nursery bed so the roots are better developed. It has taken the loss on the two-year seedlings that didn't survive that first transplanting. Not only that, many evergreens, especially spruces, seem to take forever to reach a height where you can imagine they might eventually become trees. After seven years, Colorado blue spruce may be only a foot high. By choosing the oldest and paying the slight premium, you are still getting seedling prices with the hope of having something to show within a few years.

8-4. Saplings Are for Most Gardeners

In between large specimens and seedlings are plants usually described as saplings when they are deciduous trees. These often range between six and 12 feet tall. Planted in a favorable location they will make rapid growth after the first summer and within three to seven years, depending on the kind and the location, will offer summer shade and a true tree appearance. Prices are moderate. Depending on variety they may run from about $10 to $20. They can be handled by the home gardener without any more equipment than a spade, garden hose and a hammer to drive in a stake.

Comparable evergreens will run around the same price range and will be sold either by height, which will likely run from two to four feet on upright kinds, or, in the case of spreading kinds, by spread, which will be from one to 2-1/2 feet. These are large enough to produce an immediate effect, and

Yellow *"Belvidere"* and orange *"High Society"* are among the tallest and stateliest tulips. *(Photo by Malak)*

old enough for their slowest growing years to be behind them. After it reaches three feet, for example, spruce will likely put on six to 12 inches or more a year. This growth will be in girth as well as in height so there is a rapid annual increase from this point.

8-5. Bringing Them Back Alive

It is possible to take trees from natural surroundings: those growing on your own property out of town, those from a road allowance that will be sprayed or bulldozed anyway, and extra plants given to you by a friend or neighbor, here or from another location. Unless you are sure that it is legal to remove the trees or have them given to you legally, beware. Farm fields and wood lots belong to someone. Young trees are not yours for the taking without explicit permission.

A favorite story, since it provides poetic justice for the culprit, was of a city slicker driving north on a superhighway, looking for a tree he could remove to his city lot. He began to eye the evergreens planted at the side of the highway, and stopping at what he thought was an inconspicuous place, dug one out and put it in his trunk. He turned at the next cloverleaf, returned home and planted his ''find'' on the lawn.

The only trouble was his actions had been spotted and his licence number taken. He barely finished planting when the highway patrol car showed up at his driveway. He was charged, found guilty, and sentenced to go to a nursery, buy a comparable specimen that was balled and burlapped, and replant it under police supervision in the hole he'd left at the side of the road. It would be only just if the one he stole expired on his front lawn.

Lifting a tree from the edge of the highway, or anywhere else is not usually successful, unless you follow some of the rules of the game.

The time to transplant deciduous trees (those that drop their leaves in fall) is before

there is any leaf growth in spring, or after leaves turn color or the first killing frost in fall (whichever comes first). The time to transplant evergreens is in early spring as soon as you can get a spade in the ground, or around Labor Day. The time is not auspicious in midsummer when you are on vacation and see a seedling that you just can't resist. Resist!

Trees can be moved in leaf successfully, but only with careful preparation. Ideally this should start with root pruning the year before. Do this by plunging a round-mouth spade full depth into the ground around the tree. Complete a semicircle. This severs all roots past the point of the spade entry. Water and fertilize over the summer. In the fall, repeat the process to complete the circle. This pruning causes the tree to produce a good many new roots directly under the trunk.

Lift the tree the following spring, digging it out on the line of the root-pruning circle, but keeping all the soil together and around the ball of roots under the trunk. Wrap the ball in some sort of material that will hold it together – nurseries usually use burlap and rope.

Keep the earth moist in the burlap and make the move as quickly as possible. The sooner the plant goes back in the ground, the better. Plant at the same depth it stood before.

Is all this trouble really necessary? Yes, if you want your work to count for something and not take a high risk of failure.

People gleefully describe the beautiful trees they ''yanked'' out of a wild location and moved successfully to a city or suburban garden. Some try to make the story even better by suggesting they did it in the midst of a July heat wave. Maybe so. But if it did live it was by pure fluke and in 100 repetitions it wouldn't happen again.

Other gardeners ask how they can transplant from the wild successfully because they have brought down dozens of trees from the cottage lot over the years and none has been successfully transplanted.

Make sure you get a tree that is suited to its new conditions. Trees taken from swamps seldom do well on dry, sandy soils, and vice versa. Some kinds simply don't do well in

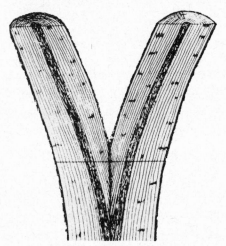

V-shaped Fork. Inner wood fibers do not unite as trunks grow in diameter.

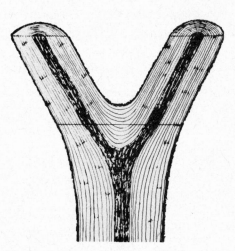

U-shaped Fork. Shows strong arrangement of wood elements.

Trees whose trunks have grown in the shape of a V are hazardous.

These hoop petticoat narcissuses are startlingly beautiful. (Photo by Malak)

cities. The beautiful eastern white pine doesn't take to city smog or dry, exposed locations.

Tamarack (larch) comes out in leaf very early in spring and must be moved before that, a difficult task if you are transplanting from north to south.

Another factor to consider is that many trees in the wild are misshapen with all the branches on one side and sometimes with the roots formed the same way. These don't have the symmetry of a nursery-grown tree, and will take years to look good as a specimen, if ever.

The size of the tree you try to move is important, too. In general, smaller sizes transplant better than larger ones do, and there is a better chance they will grow straighter and have balanced shapes. The larger the tree, the bigger the root system and the less chance you'll get it all. On the other hand, one-year seedlings are too small. They

For fiery early fall color, nothing matches the Amur river maple – and it is suitable for small properties.

take forever to grow and they have little stored vitality. Two to four-year-old trees do best. In evergreens this would probably be six to 10 inches tall; in deciduous trees, 18 inches to three or four feet.

And finally, the baby tree you bring back so proudly may grow to be a nuisance on a small property. Forest giants have no place on tiny lots.

8-6. Stick with Nurseries

Nursery-grown trees are pruned and cultivated for good shape and a compact root system so that they will be fairly easy to transplant. They are often available in selections chosen for, say, uniform growth, good fall leaf coloring, larger, more colorful or more reliable flowers. The nurseryman is available for information on planting and to give you an idea of the best location, soil requirements and the ultimate size of the tree. There is usually a choice of sizes available at different prices, and a guarantee. Some nurseries also offer planting services so that if your budget can stand it, you only need to choose and the nursery does the rest.

To give an example, you decide you want a spruce tree. Those available in the wild may be limited to one kind of spruce. But a good nursery will offer several kinds, from native trees to the much-favored Colorado blue spruce and its varieties. There are slow-growing kinds such as Black Hills spruce, semi-dwarfs such as Alberta, and weeping and low forms such as weeping blue spruce or nest spruce.

Another example could be made with the maple. You might be tempted to take on a self-sown seedling of *Acer negundo,* sometimes called "box elder". This is a valuable tree to hold down soil in severe climates and tough, exposed locations where few other trees will grow, but in more favored areas and in backyard gardens it is a second-rate specimen and a nuisance to your neighbors, since it self-seeds prolifically.

Nor would a silver maple or even a sugar maple, so glorious in a maple forest, park or large estate, be suitable to a small city lot. But there are other maples with narrow upright growth, or short spreading heads that get along in less space and still have fall color. There is even a shrub maple with bright fall color — the Amur river maple — that is suitable for small properties. It is also hardy in the north and midwest. The number of kinds of trees is great, and you owe it to yourself and your garden to investigate, eventually choosing the ones that suit you and your garden best.

Defining the Areas: Fences and Hedges

The open look in landscaping is currently popular and there's a feeling that to close off a property is to shut the neighbors out. Yet, as the speaker in Robert Frost's poem "Mending Wall" quotes his neighbor, "good fences make good neighbors."

9-1. Kinds of Fences

There is no doubt that some situations call for nothing less than a secure fence. And even those who abhor fences in the front garden like to keep the back one fenced off. Whether for general security, to stop foot traffic and shortcutting, to keep dogs in or out, there certainly are times when either a clipped hedge or a fence (or both) are the only answer.

Fences alone are the most formal separation of property there is, particularly if the fence is made of chain link, is institutional and not very attractive. There are times when it seems the only choice. It is the most people-proof of all ordinary home fencing, and fills the bill when an area has to be secured against trespassers. If the metal posts are set in concrete below the frost line, it is very long-lasting and untippable.

Somewhat more attractive is galvanized scroll-top fencing, either painted green or covered with green plastic. It is not so people-proof as the chain link kind. In fact, small people climbing it will soon bend the scrolls down and make them unsightly unless you build it with a top rail or pole to provide support for the scroll.

Farm fencing or chicken wire on posts is neither attractive nor effective in keeping unwanted visitors out.

Board fences are much more attractive although more expensive and more difficult to construct. A simple, low fence designed merely to mark off a property line can be made with a single running board on cut-off cedar poles. To make it higher, cut the posts longer and add another running board as necessary.

For more privacy and a stronger deterrent to climbers, use wide horizontal boards on alternate sides of four-by-four cedar posts. These provide a maximum of privacy consistent with their open nature that allows air to pass freely through. Stains can be used so the fence looks natural and plantings spotted along it help tie it into the garden almost as if it belonged there. Unfortunately it is easy to climb.

A variation on this is the basket weave type where the horizontal boards go alternately on one side of the posts and on the other. This tends to soften the rectangular lines and provide a woven texture. But it, too, is quite climbable. If that's a problem you might

This palisade fence makes an ideal background for high zinnias, medium geraniums and low ageratum.

consider a solid board fence with the boards running either horizontally or vertically, or the palisade type with small cedar poles set vertically into the ground. These can be reinforced with one or more rails of cedar running horizontally. This is expensive and a lot of work to install, but makes a luxury fence that blends into the garden, especially if the cedars are left to age naturally without paint or stain.

Many suburban gardeners are buying up old cedar rails from abandoned farm fences to try to recreate them on small properties. But rail fences were designed to keep cattle in, not people out and so are ineffective for that. Also, they seem pretentious, especially

on a small lot where their heavy look seems inappropriate.

Plastics seem to intrude on our lives almost everywhere and plastic fences have made their appearance, but most plastic becomes as brittle as glass in winter and it doesn't take much to shatter it.

In a different category are the plastic panels designed to provide privacy especially in dense townhouse or condominium housing. They are made of translucent material to let in light, but unfortunately they come in gaudy colors. They do not stand up to heavy wind and many people find out to their sorrow they are more trouble than they are worth.

Wooden picket fences are rarely seen any

A perfect example of how to use flowers in mass plantings: in the foreground are "JanBos" hyacinths; behind them, "Ballet" tulips and "Insurpassable" daffodils. (Photo by Malak)

The kind of plant chosen for a hedge depends on its location, its purpose, and the ease with which it can be kept in bounds.

more. However some lumberyards offer them in prefabricated panels you can quickly attach to posts and two-by-four rails. They make an attractive fence especially for a small garden and their smooth exterior and pointed tops discourage climbers. From the inside they are a perfect backdrop for shrubs and roses.

If you decide a fence is necessary, check with your local building department to see if there are bylaws relating to fence heights. In some areas heights are restricted; in others you must get consent of a neighbor who shares the property line. But it is also possible that the neighbor is responsible for half the cost of putting a fence up.

9-2. Nature's Fence

Some plants not only will grow well close to others, but stand up to a regular shearing that rigidly maintains their height and width. Gardeners soon learned to make use of them as boundary markers, divisions within a larger garden and as windbreaks and snow stoppers. They provide a formal ending to a property line while at the same time offering a softer, more natural look than fences.

As with other plantings in the garden, hedge plants may be deciduous or evergreen, have varying leaf textures and sizes and range in height from one or two feet to 12 feet or more. The kind of plant used for the hedge should be chosen on the basis of its location and purpose and the ease with which it can be kept in bounds.

Two examples come to mind of plants that are not suitable as hedges on city lots: Chinese elm and multiflora rose. The former is an extremely vigorous tree that grows eventually to 45 feet. It must be pruned repeatedly during a season to be kept within bounds, and tends to get very short of leaves around the base. The rose becomes a thicket that is too painful to prune and too widespreading for any lot short of acreage.

A good hedge plant is one that, pruned properly, will keep thick foliage to its base, doesn't have so many thorns you can't get near it, and does not require constant pruning. Add one requirement: its foliage should be small enough to be able to stand shearing so it doesn't look cut in half.

9-3. Fast-Growing or Slow-Growing

Most people are in a hurry and the idea of a fast-growing hedge appeals to them. Unfortunately the kind of plant, like Chinese elm, that does grow very swiftly, is completely unsuitable after the first few years and requires far more maintenance than most home gardeners are prepared to give.

The ideal hedge plant grows very slowly so that very little attention is needed and even if you miss pruning in one season, it won't get away from you. Unfortunately this means that you either have to wait a long time to get the privacy you are looking for, or you have to buy very expensive, mature plants to set out.

In general, deciduous plants grow higher faster than evergreen types. However, you have to balance the faster growth against the fact that the privacy disappears with the leaves in fall, and there may be as many as seven months of the year when the hedge appears to be a bunch of dead sticks, as one gardener put it.

Among evergreens, there is a choice between the flat-leafed, such as Eastern white cedar or yew, needle evergreens, such as pine and spruce, and broad-leafed kinds (in the very mildest climates), such as laurel cherry, holly and boxwood (for medium mild climates). Boxwood, and in particular Korean boxwood and hybrids between it and the English boxwood, are excellent for garden divisions, for low hedges along pathways, in front of foundation plantings, and to edge a rose garden. They grow extremely slowly, usually need only touch-up pruning and rarely grow over three feet high.

Needle evergreens were sometimes used for high fences in years gone by, but they are not recommended for anything lower than 12 feet and not even then without reservations. Neither spruce nor pine can initiate new growth from old wood; they have to be allowed to grow out, becoming broader and broader, and the inside needles die and drop off.

Yew (Japanese, hybrid or English where hardy) makes a fine, medium-height evergreen hedge that will do very well in shade and even in city gardens where air pollution is a problem. It is very slow-growing and therefore very expensive to buy in any quantity.

Hemlock (Canada and western) makes a fine-leafed bright evergreen hedge that stands up to clipping and can be kept moderately high. It too becomes very expensive when bought in any quantities from a nursery.

White cedar (*Thuja occidentalis* in the east and false cypress or chamaecyparis in the west) is probably the best compromise between costs, rate of growth and ease in clipping and growing the plants. They will get along in relatively dry soil, sand or clay, but prefer moist locations. They can be bought as seedlings, as volunteer plants from farmers' fields, or as nursery-grown specimens at relatively minor cost.

9-4. Deciduous Hedges

As with evergreens, choice of material for a

The flowers in this colorful, well-planned garden repeat the straight lines of the fence and walks. (Photo by Malak)

deciduous hedge depends on the eventual height and the leaf texture. For extremely dwarf deciduous hedges, use Arctic willow which will grow almost as broad as it does high. A slightly higher, flowering hedge is cinquefoil.

For low hedges try pigmy caragana, alpine currant (one of the best, and it stands up to air pollution), dwarf honeysuckle, various euonymus, spirea, and gooseberries which make a thicket and bear fruit.

Among medium-height material, privet has long been a favorite hedge plant in the east and caragana in the midwest. But each has drawbacks. Privet is subject to a number of insect infestations and caragana tends to have thin foliage.

For medium hedges some native plants are excellent, such as buffalo berry, cranberry, chokecherry (especially the Shubert purple-leafed), Russian olive, honeysuckle (on the prairies) and shrub roses other than multi-flora.

For tall hedges, be prepared for stepladder pruning. There are the Chinese elms mentioned earlier, lilacs, serviceberries (Saskatoons and the eastern Juneberry or shadbush), beech, hawthorn (for an impenetrable thicket), tall honeysuckle and crabapples grown to a bush shape.

9-5. Annual Plants for Hedges

A good, conventional woody hedge takes a long time to grow properly — from three or four years for Chinese elm to 10 or more for yews, depending on the size plant you start with. And it is a rather permanent fixture of your garden. Once mature, it can't be moved and the only choice if you don't like it where it is, is to remove it.

Marigolds are suitable for spot gardens or for a hedge – unlike most hedge plants, they may be grown from seed to maturity in one season.

If you like the idea of a hedge but think you may change your mind about its location, or if you like the idea of a hedge in summer only, particularly one that flowers or has attractive foliage colors and don't want to take on the regular pruning job a permanent hedge requires, consider an annual hedge — a hedge made up of plants that can be grown from seed to maturity in one season.

Probably marigolds would be the first choice. You can grow them from seed or started plants. There is a group called the "Jubilee series" that grows to a uniform height of 1-1/2 to 2 feet and blooms continuously. Happy Face is a newer member of the group with earlier flowers. Other marigolds run from six inches to three feet.

Summer cypress grows to three feet or more in a season. Individual globe-shaped plants intertwine when grown together and the foliage is so dense you can't see through it. It turns bright red in fall.

Other annual possibilities are castor oil bean plant (the beans or seeds are poisonous), sunflowers (from three feet to 12), giant snapdragons, dwarf dahlias, scarlet sage, cleome (spider plant), and ornamental grasses.

9-6. Combine Fence and Hedge

Sometimes it's imperative to get a closure round your property to keep foot traffic or dogs out, but you'd really rather have a hedge. There is no reason not to have your cake and eat it too. Build the fence immediately for the protection you need, and then plant the hedge plants, whether permanent or annual, on your side of the fence line. In a short time the plants will hide the fence from your eyes, and eventually, with an evergreen hedge, from the street or a neighbor as well. In

Rocks are as much a part of nature as plants and earth, so it is not surprising that these boulders fit in well with plantings of petunias.

time the fence may not be self-supporting from the rotting of the posts, but if the hedge is permanent it will support the fence for many more years. By that time the hedge should be so dense as to make the fence unnecessary.

9-7. The Informal Hedge

A permanent planting can be made along the property line to mark it off without clipping it into a formal hedge. This used to be called a "hedgerow" and can be made up of trees, shrubs or evergreens all of a kind, or an even less formal intermix of flowering shrubs, trees and evergreens allowed to grow naturally. Typical of such plantings are rows of maples, pines or spruces along farm roads and to separate pastures. The idea could be adapted easily to a large suburban property using full-size trees, and to smaller properties by using small or dwarf trees, evergreens and shrubs. Less formal still would be the spot planting of the occasional tree, shrub or evergreen along the property line. It would leave no doubt as to where the line was, but at the same time not give a shut-in or -out feeling and allow lots of open space between.

There is evidence in this garden of detailed planning: low flowers fronting tall ones, tulips in various stages of development for longer-lasting color, and plantings at different levels to provide interest. (Photo by Malak)

10 Brick, Stone, Concrete and Wood

Rock and stones are as much part of nature as plants and earth. In fact, as we've seen, the rocks and stones preceded all the rest and it was the breakdown of rock that produced soil in the first place.

In Japan, stones, sand and boulders, alone or in combination, sometimes make up the entire "planting" of a garden. There are few streams, lakes or ocean shores that don't have sand, rocks or boulders somewhere

Brick walls are elegant and expensive; they are one of the features we admire in old world gardens.

Brick walks have a soft look that appears natural among plants.

The stone floor and brick wall of this patio garden blend perfectly with the plantings.

around. In nature these are often mixed in varying proportions and interlaced with every kind of plant from wildflowers through ferns to trees and evergreens.

Thus it is no accident that sand, gravel and rock surfaces are an acceptable part of our gardens. We use them to construct buildings, for paths, retaining walls and sometimes for driveways. They make handsome steps and steppingstones, edging for pools, garden paths and patio paving.

Also formed of the earth, clay brick, though manufactured in rectangular shapes, also appears natural when used among plants. It has a soft look as path, patio and driveway paving, and a brick wall or fence, almost prohibitively expensive due to the labor involved, is one of the charms we admire in old-world gardens.

Brick and stone need to be set in a minimum six-inch-deep layer of fine sand when used as paving so they won't heave with frost, and so you can level the sand easily before laying the paving. This is particularly important with slabs or pieces of stone that are not level on the bottom; it is quite easy to arrange a bed to take the stone in sand so the stone remains level, but virtually impossible in heavy soil, especially clay.

The sand insures good drainage and helps the paving to dry out quickly after a rain. It also decreases the chances of heaving from frost action during the alternate freezing and thawing in winter. Any movement that does occur can easily be readjusted the following spring.

In the interests of neatness and preventing weeds from growing between bricks or stones, some people like to mortar the spaces. This works if you can use mortar neatly without staining the paving material, but is subject to frost cracking and thus requires a more elaborate repair procedure each year. It's a good deal easier to use some sand put aside from the load that went in under the paving. Let it dry and then sift it down between the stones or bricks, using a corn broom. Use the hose if necessary to wash it in and help pack it.

A little weeding now and then over the season will keep weeds and weedgrasses at bay. Or you could even sow it to grass, running the mower over it now and then to keep it trim. In some cases where there is not much foot traffic, you might want to plant it to some heat-loving plant such as portulaca, thyme, hens and chickens, or a sedum.

To make a really frost-secure, mortared patio, you would need to lay a heavy layer of concrete on top of a gravel underbed, and then set the bricks or stones into the not-yet-set concrete. Follow by mortaring between.

Brick or stone walls should have footings below the frost line to prevent serious damage — even toppling over — as a result of alternate freezing and thawing of the ground. This is a great deal of work if you do it yourself or a good deal of expense if you hire it done. But if stone or brick walls are for you, there is nothing that looks as good.

There is a new product on the market you might want to consider for paving: bricks made so that they interlock. They can be laid in patterns that please you, need no mortar to stick together, and produce a professional-looking job with a little care in preparing the base in the beginning.

10-1. Using Crushed Rock

Crushed rock is a marvellous material to absorb weight, say of vehicles, without allowing them to sink into the ground. It does this by spreading it over a wide area from one piece of crushed stone to another. But it has a raw look, and unless extremely finely crushed (which then takes away from its ability to support weight) it is very hard to walk on. Ideally it is used as the base for something finer in driveways, and for drainage over tile beds, by and in window wells where the window is below grade and might otherwise collect water.

Once the crushed rock has settled and been replenished as necessary on driveways and paths, small round stones make a fine surface treatment; so does shale, plain or colored. Shale packs to a firm surface, yet still lets water pass through to the earth below instead of running it all off to storm sewers as do the more impervious kinds of paving mentioned below.

White or colored medium-size unbroken stones are often used or suggested as a mulch among evergreens where they are attractive and have the advantage of letting rain or irrigation pass freely through (as contrasted with organic mulches such as dried grass clippings, partly worked compost, peat moss). Their disadvantages are their weight which makes it very hard to move them or change the pattern (or to haul them in, in the first place) and the temptation they present to children to use them for ammunition or building blocks.

10-2. Rock Gardens

Construction of rock gardens by amateurs too often turns into simply a rock pile with some plants stuck here and there among them. A rubble pile is not a garden and can't really be made to look like one. So stifle the urge to use the assortment of many-colored stones or boulders the builder buried in the soil under your lawn and garden, or the rocks you pick up on vacations, unless they are matching, and unless you can arrange them in a natural manner.

To become a garden a pile of rocks must be arranged with each other and with the sur-

White medium-sized unbroken stones are often used as a mulch among evergreens.

rounding garden so that they appear to be a natural outcropping of stone through the earth's surface. Before you start, get some ideas by visiting places where there are natural outcroppings, or where professionals have constructed them in parks or private gardens. The kind of rock most suitable is the porous type that holds moisture and allows mosses and lichens to grow on their surface. Weathered and worn rock looks more natural than the fresh, shiny surface of boulders just uncovered, and for amateur construction, rocks with at least one flat side are easier to arrange and work with than those that are relatively round.

Sedimentary stones such as limestone, sandstone, tufa and shale are the preferred stone to use, and the more weatherbeaten and full of holes, the better. There is an artificial lightweight stone available that looks as good as pocked limestone. But limestone is usually easy to find, cheap, easy to split or break and very congenial to many plants, shrubs and evergreens. Whatever kind you do decide to use, stick to it. Start mixing various kinds and colors and you get back to the rock pile look.

In natural rock outcroppings, most of the mass of rock is under the soil, and a rock garden should be constructed the same way. Spotting of rocks here and there in the surface soil achieves only the stony look of glacial droppings that make for bad farmland.

Lay out the rock garden area with strings and stakes. Excavate under and back from that line. Lay down a layer of broken stones and chips under and back (into the hill if you are building on a hill) as underdrainage. On that, place a layer of stone chips and sand. On this, place some topsoil into which you set the major, supporting rocks, in front of and on top of which the exposed rocks will sit. These should lean back into the topsoil which is also filled in around them. No more than half of these surface rocks should actually be above the soil level to insure their stability and so that rain hits their surface rather than the soil, which washes out. The effect on the surface should be roughly that of shingles on a roof, but the line should be slightly irregular and broken, not perfectly rectangular. Again this imitates natural outcroppings where frost, wind and rain have broken the rock edges and weathered them (as this happened, spaces in the rock filled with bits of plant remains which turned to soil and began to support plant life).

There are many variations on the rock garden theme, such as ledge steps, boulder gardens and low-ledge gardens. All use the basic principle that the greatest mass of stone, like that of icebergs, lies below the surface.

To build any of these gardens on level ground requires either a retaining wall (see below), or a rearrangement of the grade of land in the garden. Earlier we discussed a raised garden, or transforming a yard with a slight grade so that there were two levels and all the grade difference occurred at one place. This would be an ideal location for a rock garden.

10-3. Dry Wall Construction

While a lifetime, rigid retaining wall can be built only of mortared stones or bricks on a foundation with a crushed rock base below the frost line, there are a number of ways you can build a dry wall, that is, a wall of stone without mortar that depends on the balance of weight for its stability.

Because the stones are not fixed in position, slight shiftings from frost action will not matter. The soil and sand packing behind and between the stones may have to be replaced or added to occasionally, but the wall will hold. There are well-constructed dry walls still useful and in place decades after being built.

Start by laying out the dimensions and excavating behind. The largest, flattest, widest stones should be at the base, and the stones should be slightly tilted backwards to tie into the soil behind. Again, as with the rock garden, most of the stone will be hidden and the weight of the rocks above will tend to push the rocks below into the soil behind, making them more stable. Place wet soil over them and compact it. Also place wet soil behind the

A dry wall (a stone wall built without mortar) should have the largest, flattest stones at the base, and they should be tilted slightly to the rear.

rock layer so it is firm and rises to meet the wet soil placed on top. Repeat this pattern with progressively smaller rocks as you near the top level so the face of the wall recedes until you reach the top. There the stones, still set so they angle back into the soil behind, are half-covered with soil. This soil should be continuous with the earth packed behind the wall.

The end of the wall, or its corner, presents a problem in that stones may be dislodged if you bump them or if they are particularly exposed to weather. These corners not only have to angle back from the exposed face on one side, but on the exposed end as well. It may be easier to mortar them even though frost may crack it so you have to remortar occasionally.

The soil layer in between the rocks may be minimal so it doesn't actually show from the face. Or you can make it thicker so you can set plants in the small spaces between the rocks.

There is a short-cut method of making a dry wall using hollow or interlocking concrete blocks. Start with a crushed rock base of six inches or more and place the blocks along the line you want. Step the next layer, using a half-block to start so full blocks cover the separation between blocks of the line below, but placing the blocks so the hole in the center is continuous. Repeat until the wall is as high as you need it.

Then drive steel T-bars (used for fencing) down through the holes in the blocks at each end of the wall, and one or more in the middle. These should go through the crushed rock base and several feet into the soil below, and be level with the top surface of the blocks. They will hold the wall firm against considerable soil pressure from behind.

Using cement or cement mortar, cap the top, perhaps setting attractive stones into the mortar to give the wall a more natural appearance (there are cement blocks available with pebbled or stone faces, and with fluting that makes them look more like stone). Attractive stones can also be placed on the stepped ends before mortaring.

10-4. Cement and Asphalt

Ordinary cast concrete is a practical workhorse in garden construction, extremely valuable for foundation work, but essentially sterile and unattractive as a surface material. Because it is relatively cheap, easy to produce and plastic when wet so it can be moulded, or trowelled to suit the shape required, there is a great temptation to use it instead of more attractive materials that are not so convenient.

But there are things you can do with concrete that help it to blend into garden settings better. Perhaps the most attractive effect is achieved by brushing the surface with a wet broom or whisk just after the first set when the concrete is firm but not yet hard. This is called "exposed aggregate", and is as attractive as the stones you used to make the material in the first place.

By using medusa cement and white sand you can get an almost pure white concrete if that suits your needs. And various dyes are available to use in the mix so the finished concrete will be a muted, dull gray, red, green or yellow.

It is also possible to make a lightweight mixture, such as for casting planter shapes, by substituting vermiculite or perlite for half the sand. The casting will be relatively soft so that it can be chiselled with designs, yet plenty sturdy enough to grow plants in and be moved here and there for many years. Molds should be well greased with motor oil or paraffin so you don't damage the casting in removing it. A mixture that works well is one part portland cement, two parts clean, sharp sand, two parts vermiculite and one part water.

Of all the garden building materials, asphalt is the least attractive. Even if you paint it, it never looks like a natural part of the landscape. In driveways it absorbs (and deteriorates from) spilled motor oil, and unless made with the same foundation preparations as

Using a tree stump for a bird bath is one way of taking advantage of the natural elements of your garden.

Wood rounds make a good paving material for garden paths.

concrete, develops splits and cracks that support as many weeds as a stone driveway does. Its chief advantage is that it makes snow shovelling easier.

10-5. Wood In the Garden

It's a tossup whether wood or stone was the first building material used by mankind. But there is no argument about whether wood is natural or not. Though increasingly expensive and becoming rare in large sizes, wood is still a prime material for many garden uses.

Left to weather to natural dark and silver grays, as with the increasingly popular weathered barn boards and rails from fences, or preserved with a natural-looking preservative-stain, it fits in everywhere as decking, steps from one level to another, for retaining

walls of pegged logs, as fence posts and board fences, in plant containers, for arbors, lathing and greenhouses, gazebos, garden furniture and even as paving in the form of wood rounds or chips (which also make a good mulch to conserve moisture around plants and to discourage weeds).

Some kinds of wood are especially resistant to decay. These include California redwood, Eastern white cedar, false cypress, larch, juniper and locust, and so are first choice where there is dampness or where the wood is to be in contact with the earth. Even so you get longer life from the wood by painting it with or soaking it in wood preservative.

Wood fits into the garden picture the least when it is covered with a high-gloss paint in a bright color. Natural wood colors are best and stains look better than enamels. If you must choose the latter, use a low-gloss product, and preferably white, which blends with or provides a background for plants without competing with them for attention.

A hedge may be used in combination with a wood fence to ensure privacy.

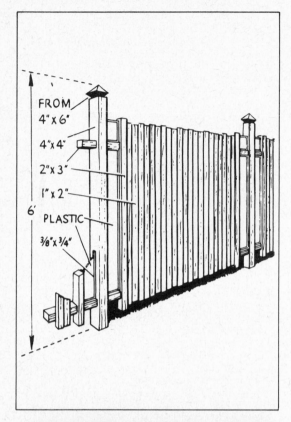

FROM
4" x 6"
4" x 4"
2" x 3"
1" x 2"
PLASTIC
³⁄₈" x ³⁄₄"
6'

These fences are attractive as well as functional.

HIGH FENCE DESIGNS

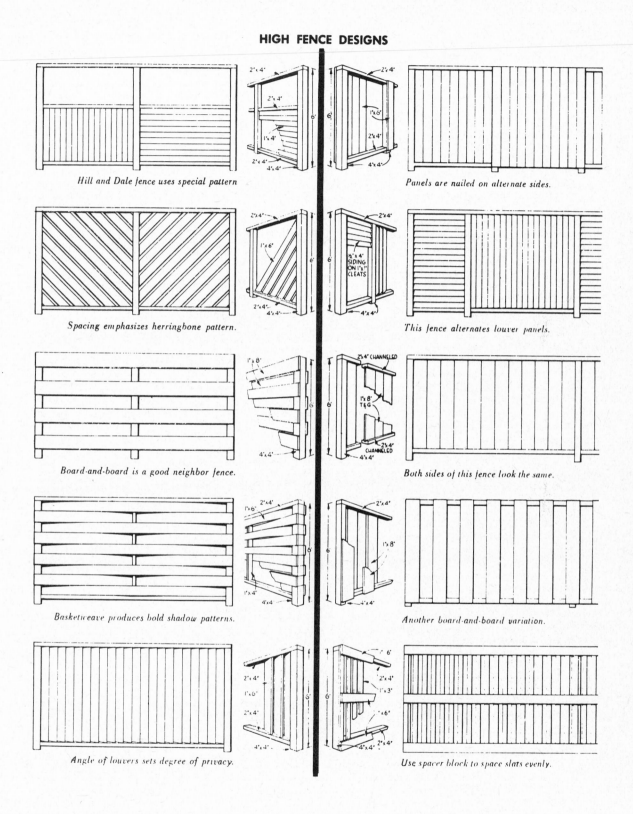

Hill and Dale fence uses special pattern

Panels are nailed on alternate sides.

Spacing emphasizes herringbone pattern.

This fence alternates louver panels.

Board-and-board is a good neighbor fence.

Both sides of this fence look the same.

Basketweave produces bold shadow patterns.

Another board-and-board variation.

Angle of louvers sets degree of privacy.

Use spacer block to space slats evenly.

Use garden-grade redwood for most of these as it is weather-resistant like all redwood, and the more rustic, knotty wood is less expensive.

Appendix

TULIP GROWTH CYCLE

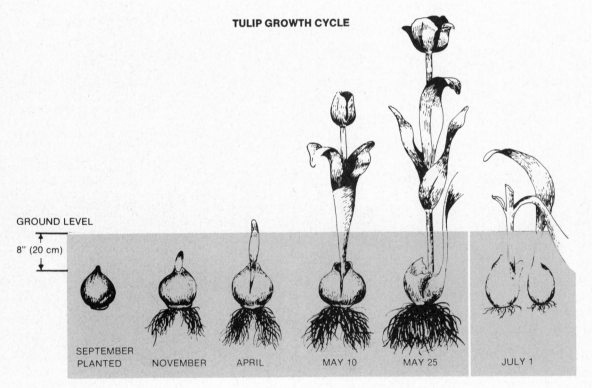

GROUND LEVEL

8" (20 cm)

SEPTEMBER PLANTED   NOVEMBER   APRIL   MAY 10   MAY 25   JULY 1

Chart from "Flowering Bulbs for Canadian Gardens", courtesy of Agriculture Canada

TYPES OF BULBS

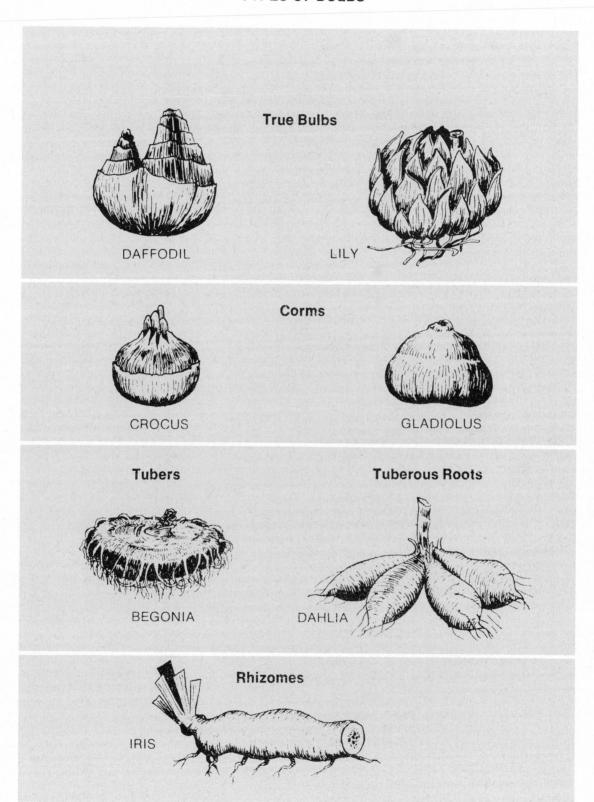

True Bulbs

DAFFODIL

LILY

Corms

CROCUS

GLADIOLUS

Tubers

Tuberous Roots

BEGONIA

DAHLIA

Rhizomes

IRIS

Chart from "Flowering Bulbs for Canadian Gardens", courtesy of Agriculture Canada

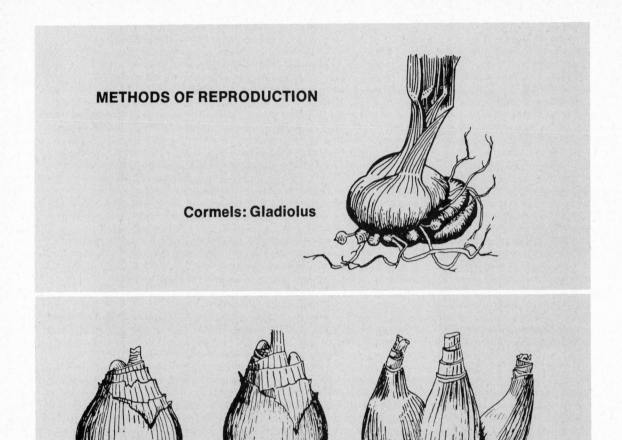

METHODS OF REPRODUCTION

Cormels: Gladiolus

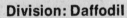

Division: Daffodil

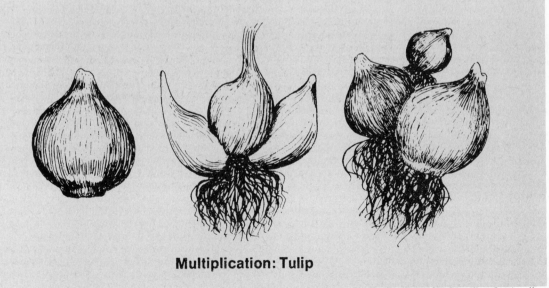

Multiplication: Tulip

Chart from "Flowering Bulbs for Canadian Gardens",
courtesy of Agriculture Canada

METRIC EQUIVALENTS

LENGTH

inch	= 2.54 cm	millimetre	= 0.039 in.
foot	= 0.3048 m	centimetre	= 0.394 in.
yard	= 0.914 m	decimetre	= 3.937 in.
mile	= 1.609 km	metre	= 3.28 ft
		kilometre	= 0.621 mile

AREA

square inch	= 6.452 cm²	cm²	= 0.155 sq in.
square foot	= 0.093 m²	m²	= 1.196 sq yd
square yard	= 0.836 m²	km²	= 0.386 sq mile
square mile	= 2.59 km²	ha	= 2.471 ac
acre	= 0.405 ha		

VOLUME (DRY)

cubic inch	= 16.387 cm³	cm³	= 0.061 cu in.
cubic foot	= 0.028 m³	m³	= 31.338 cu ft
cubic yard	= 0.765 m³	hectolitre	= 2.8 bu
bushel	= 36.368 litres	m³	= 1.308 cu yd
board foot	= 0.0024 m³		

VOLUME (LIQUID)

fluid ounce (Imp)	= 28.412 ml	litre	= 35.2 fluid oz
pint	= 0.568 litre	hectolitre	= 26.418 gal
gallon	= 4.546 litres		

WEIGHT

ounce	= 28.349 g	gram	= 0.035 oz avdp
pound	= 453.592 g	kilogram	= 2.205 lb avdp
hundredweight (Imp)	= 45.359 kg	tonne	= 1.102 short ton
ton	= 0.907 tonne		

PROPORTION

1 gal/acre	= 11.232 litres/ha	1 litre/ha	= 14.24 fluid oz/acre
1 lb/acre	= 1.120 kg/ha	1 kg/ha	= 14.5 oz avdp/acre
1 lb/sq in.	= 0.0702 kg/cm²	1 kg/cm²	= 14.227 lb/sq in.
1 bu/acre	= 0.898 hl/ha	1 hl/ha	= 1.112 bu/acre

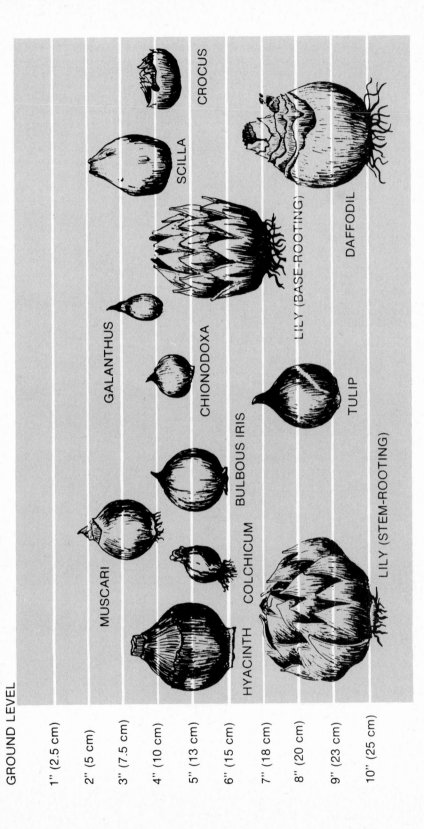

PLANT IN FALL

GROUND LEVEL

1" (2.5 cm)

2" (5 cm)

3" (7.5 cm)

4" (10 cm)

5" (13 cm)

6" (15 cm)

7" (18 cm)

8" (20 cm)

9" (23 cm)

10" (25 cm)

CROCUS

SCILLA

GALANTHUS

CHIONODOXA

BULBOUS IRIS

MUSCARI

COLCHICUM

HYACINTH

LILY (BASE-ROOTING)

DAFFODIL

TULIP

LILY (STEM-ROOTING)

Chart from "Flowering Bulbs for Canadian Gardens", courtesy of Agriculture Canada

PLANT IN SPRING

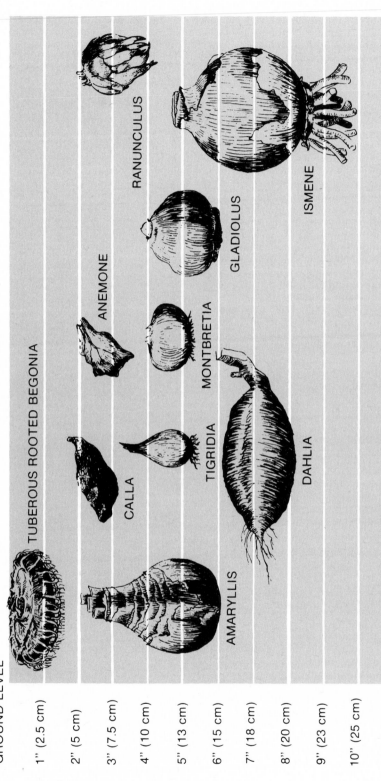

GROUND LEVEL

1" (2.5 cm)

2" (5 cm)

3" (7.5 cm)

4" (10 cm)

5" (13 cm)

6" (15 cm)

7" (18 cm)

8" (20 cm)

9" (23 cm)

10" (25 cm)

TUBEROUS ROOTED BEGONIA

ANEMONE

CALLA

MONTBRETIA

TIGRIDIA

RANUNCULUS

GLADIOLUS

ISMENE

DAHLIA

AMARYLLIS

Chart from "Flowering Bulbs for Canadian Gardens", courtesy of Agriculture Canada

COMMON AND GENERIC NAMES OF BULBS

Common Name	Generic Name
acidanthera	Acidanthera
aconite, winter-	Eranthis
allium	Allium
amaryllis	Hippeastrum
amaryllis, Hall-	Lycoris
anemone	Anemone
begonia	Begonia
belladonna-lily	Amaryllis
Bengal-lily	Crinum
blackberry-lily	Belamcanda
bluebell, English	Scilla
bluebell, Siberian-	Ixiolirion
bluebell, Spanish	Scilla
calla, yellow	Zantedeschia
camassia	Camassia
candlestick lily	Lilium
canna	Canna
cape-hyacinth	Galtonia
checkered-lily	Fritillaria
chives	Allium
coral drops	Bessera
corn-lily	Ixia
crocus	Crocus
crocus, fall-	Colchicum
crocus, Scotch	Crocus
crown imperial	Fritillaria
daffodil	Narcissus
dahlia	Dahlia
delicate-lily	Chlidanthus
dog's-tooth violet	Erythronium
Dutch iris	Iris
English bluebell	Scilla
English iris	Iris
fairy-lily, white	Zephyranthes
fall-crocus	Colchicum
false Solomon's-seal	Smilacina
foxtail-lily	Eremurus
fritillary, yellow	Fritillaria
gladiolus	Gladiolus
globe-tulip	Calochortus
glory-of-the-snow	Chionodoxa
grape-hyacinth	Muscari
Hall-amaryllis	Lycoris
Hanson's lily	Lilium
hyacinth	Hyacinthus
hyacinth, cape-	Galtonia
hyacinth, grape-	Muscari
iris	Iris
iris, Dutch	Iris
iris, English	Iris
iris, Spanish	Iris
Ismene-lily	Hymenocallis
Jack-in-the-pulpit	Arisaema
Josephine's-lily	Brunsvigia
lady tulip	Tulipa
leek, lily	Allium
lily	Lilium
lily, belladonna-	Amaryllis
lily, Bengal-	Crinum
lily, blackberry-	Belamcanda
lily, candlestick	Lilium
lily, checkered-	Fritillaria
lily, corn-	Ixia
lily, delicate-	Chlidanthus
lily, foxtail-	Eremurus
lily, Hanson's	Lilium

Common Name	Generic Name
lily, Ismene-	*Hymenocallis*
lily, Josephine's-	*Brunsvigia*
lily leek	*Allium*
lily, madonna	*Lilium*
lily, Mariposa-	*Calochortus*
lily-of-the-Nile	*Agapanthus*
lily-of-the-valley	*Convallaria*
lily, Peruvian-	*Hymenocallis*
lily, regal	*Lilium*
lily, St. Bruno's-	*Paradisea*
lily, St. James's-	*Sprekelia*
lily, snake's-head	*Fritillaria*
lily, trout-	*Erythronium*
lily, white fairy-	*Zephyranthes*
madonna lily	*Lilium*
Mariposa-lily	*Calochortus*
Mexican tiger	*Tigridia*
montbretia	*Crocosmia*
narcissus	*Narcissus*
nodding onion	*Allium*
onion, nodding	*Allium*
painted trillium	*Trillium*
paperwhite	*Narcissus*
Peruvian-lily	*Hymenocallis*
purple trillium	*Trillium*
ranunculus	*Ranunculus*
regal lily	*Lilium*
saffron, spring	*Bulbocodium*
St. Bruno's-lily	*Paradisea*
St. James's-lily	*Sprekelia*
Scotch crocus	*Crocus*
shellflower	*Tigridia*
Siberian-bluebell	*Ixiolirion*
Siberian squill	*Scilla*
snake's-head lily	*Fritillaria*
snowdrop	*Galanthus*
snowflake	*Leucojum*
snowflake, summer	*Leucojum*
Solomon's-seal	*Polygonatum*
Solomon's-seal, false	*Smilacina*
Spanish bluebell	*Scilla*
Spanish iris	*Iris*
spring beauty	*Claytonia*
spring saffron	*Bulbocodium*
squill	*Scilla*
squill, Siberian	*Scilla*
squill, striped-	*Puschkinia*
star-of-Bethlehem	*Ornithogalum*
sternbergia	*Sternbergia*
striped squill	*Puschkinia*
summer snowflake	*Leucojum*
tiger, Mexican	*Tigridia*
trillium	*Trillium*
trillium, painted	*Trillium*
trillium, purple	*Trillium*
trillium, white	*Trillium*
trout-lily	*Erythronium*
tuberose	*Polianthes*
tulip	*Tulipa*
tulip, globe-	*Calochortus*
tulip, lady	*Tulipa*
tulip, water-lily	*Tulipa*
violet, dog's-tooth	*Erythronium*
water-lily tulip	*Tulipa*
white fairy-lily	*Zephyranthes*
white trillium	*Trillium*
winter-aconite	*Eranthis*
yellow calla	*Zantedeschia*
yellow fritillary	*Fritillaria*

VEGETABLES FOR APARTMENT GARDENING

Variety	Container & Size	Fertilizer	Number of Plants
Sprite Bush Green Bean	Balcony Planter Box	One handful	Four plants.
Bush Ramano Bean Honey Gold Bush Wax Bean Blue Lake Bush Bean	---------------------------- 25 inches long by 8 inches wide by 6½ inches deep	Magamp slow release fert- ilizer (7-40-6)	Repeat sowing for continuous crops.
Spring Red Beets	Same As Above	Same As Above	Two rows, 12 plants
Baby Finger Nantes Carrots	Same As Above	Same As Above	Two rows. Thin to 3 inches apart. Sow thinly. Resow after harvest.
Champion Radish Cherry Belle Radish	Same As Above	Same As Above	Sow every two weeks for continuous supply. Don't crowd.
Buttercrunch Lettuce	Same As Above	Two handfuls Magamp slow re- lease fertili- zer (7-40-6)	Six plants. Resow after harvesting each plant.
Ebenezer Onion White Onion	Same As Above	Same As Above	In sets, plant more as onions are harvest- ed. Two rows. Onion seed must be started very early.

Variety	Container & Size	Fertilizer	Number of Plants
Green Curled Endive Full Heart Batavian Escarole	Same As Above	Same As Above	Two plants. Pick leaves for salads or harvest entire plant when mature.
Darki Parsley	Same As Above	Same As Above	Two rows with plants 3 inches apart.
Marjoram Thyme Summer Savory	Same As Above	Same As Above	One row of 6 plants 3 inches apart.
Baron Shumacher S Strawberry	Same As Above	Same As Above	Thin to 8 plants.
Tiny Tim Dwarf Tomato	Same As Above	Same As Above	Thin to 3 plants.
Stakeless Dwarf Tomato	Large Shrub Pot. 10½ inches wide by 9 inches deep	Same As Above	One Plant.
Victory Slicing Cucumber Patio Pick Cucumber	Same As Above	Same As Above	Three plants teepee staked in pot. Use Blossom Set for pol-ination if bees are not in evidence.

The soil mixture should be 2/3 commercial soil mix, plus 1/3 sand. A medium sized bag (6 lbs.) plus a shovel full of sand will fill the planter box. Slightly more will be needed for the large pot. Do not use BLOSSOM SET on any plants except the Cucumbers and Tomatoes as none of the others requires bees for pollination.

TREE HEIGHTS   Height at Maturity

Name	25-40 feet	40-80 feet	Over 80 feet
American elm			X
American holly		X	
Amur chokecherry		X	
beech			X
big-leaf linden			X
bigcone pine			X
black cherry			X
black oak			X
box elder		X	
California black oak			X
California laurel		X	
camellia (common)		X	
cherry crabapple		X	
Chinese elm		X	
Chinese juniper		X	
Chinese paper birch		X	
Chinese poplar		X	
Colorado spruce			X
common olive	X		
crabapple	X		
dawn redwood			X
dogwood (evergreen)		X	
dogwood (flowering)		X	
Douglas fir			X
Dutch elm			X
eastern black walnut			X
eastern larch		X	
eastern red cedar			X
eastern white pine			X
English elm			X
English oak			X
English walnut			X

TREE HEIGHTS   Height at Maturity

	25-40 feet	40-80 feet	Over 80 feet
euonymus	X		
European alder			X
European ash			X
European birch		X	
European larch			X
European linden			X
European mountain ash		X	
fir			X
flowering ash	X		
golden larch			X
gray birch	X		
hawthorn	X		
jack pine		X	
Japanese clethra	X		
Japanese dogwood	X		
Japanese hemlock			X
Japanese maple	X		
Japanese tree lilac	X		
Korean fir		X	
Korean mountain ash		X	
Korean pine			X
laburnum	X		
laurel	X		
laurel oak		X	
live oak		X	
mountain maple	X		
Norway maple			X

TREE HEIGHTS

Height at Maturity

	25-40 feet	40-80 feet	Over 80 feet
Oregon white oak			X
paper mulberry (common)		X	
pitch pine		X	
poplar			X
red alder		X	
red maple			X
red pine		X	
river birch			X
Russian olive	X		
Scotch elm			X
Scotch pine		X	
Siberian crabapple		X	
silver linden			X
smooth-leaved elm	X		
southern wax myrtle		X	
Spanish oak		X	
sugar maple			X
sweet bay		X	
torrey pine		X	
tulip tree			X
western hemlock			X
western red cedar		X	
white ash			X
willow oak		X	

Shrubs and vines that grow in the city

American elder
Amur river maple
andromeda
bayberry
bittersweet
Boston ivy
buckthorn
crabapple
English ivy
euonymus
forsythia
honeysuckle
hydrangea
Japanese barberry
red chokecherry
red osier dogwood
scarlet firethorn
Siberian dogwood
spirea
Virginia creeper
witch hazel

Shrubs that grow in dry soils

Amur river maple
bayberry
buckthorn
cinquefoil
common juniper
creeping juniper
evergreen euonymus
myrtle
oleander
privet
red cedar
rosemary
russet buffaloberry
Spanish broom
sumac
tamarix

Shrubs that grow in wet soils

alders
American arborvitae
bayberry
blueberry
Canada yew
dogwood
heather
mountain laurel
red osier dogwood
rosemary
serviceberry

Shrubs that give shade

alder
andromeda
camellia
chokecherry
cypress
dogwood
firethorn
holly
honeysuckle
laurel
leucothoe
mountain maple
periwinkle:
photinia
privet
serviceberry
witch hazel

Shrubs that grow in acid soils

arbutus
blueberry
bog rosemary
broom
clethra
common juniper
heath
heather
holly
laurel
leucothoe
rhododendron
serviceberry

Trees for small properties

Amur river maple
broadleaf euonymus
Canada hemlock
English holly
hawthorn
hedge maple
Japanese maple
Japanese tree lilac
locust (hybrid honey)
mountain ash
paper birch
Russian olive

QUICK FACTS ABOUT COMMON ANNUALS

The following table gives at a glance information about common annuals, including how high they grow, common use, the time the seed takes to germinate, how far apart to plant them, and other comments.

PLANT	HEIGHT (Inches)	USES	GERM. (DAYS)	SPAC-ING	NOTES
Ageratum	6-20	Edging.	5	5-10	Cut off dead flowers.
Balsam	12-18	Beds, pots, mixed garden.	10	12-14	Dislikes cold, wet; very frost-sensitive.
Calendula	14-18	Cut flowers, window garden.	10	10-14	Good in cool weather.
Celosia	16-49	Cut flowers, drying.	10	10-20	Needs rich soil.
Coreopsis	18-24	Bedding, edging.	8	10-14	Fast to flower.
Cosmos	30-48	Screen, bedding.	5	12-24	Early types best; pinch back spindly seedlings; thrive in any soil.
Gaillardia	10-20	Cut flowers, drying.	20	10-20	Doubles best.
Marigold	6-30	Bedding, cut flowers, window garden.	5	6-24	Rich soil delays blooming.
Morning glory	8-12 feet	Vine, screen.	5	24-36	Nick seeds to speed germination, sow only when soil warm.
Nasturtium	12	Bedding, edging, boxes.	8	9-12	Blooms in month from seed; needs good drainage, low fertility.
Poppy	12-16	Borders, cut flowers.	10	6-12	Hard to transplant; sow successively.
Portulaca	6-9	Bedding, edging, to hang over low walls.	10	10-12	Loves hot, dry spots; self-sows.
Scabiosa	18-36	Borders, cut flowers.	10	6-12	Needs rich, well-drained soil; cut off old flowers.
Snapdragon	6-36	Beds, borders, cutting.	15	6-24	Fine seed; pinch.
Stocks	24-39	Cut flowers, dwarfs for bedding.	5	10-12	Very fragrant, needs cool weather to flower well.
Sunflower	3-7 feet	Cut flowers, screen, seed, attract birds.	5	12-36	Use new dwarfs for any but largest garden.
Sweet pea	12-48	Cut flowers, screen.	15	8-10	Sow seeds early, need cool weather, rich soil.
Zinnia	6-36	Beds, borders, cut flowers, dwarfs for edging.	5	6-24	Thin after first bloom, removing poor-flowering plants; takes heat well but mildews in high humidity.

GUIDE TO VEGETABLE SEED PLANTING

VARIETY	INDOOR STARTS		OUTDOORS STARTS	BEST SPROUTING TEMP. (ºF)	AVG. DAYS TO SPROUT	SEEDING DEPTH/ DIST.	PLANT SPACING
	NECESSARY?	WHEN? (Wk. to last frost)	BEST TIME				
Asparagus	No	—	Late spring through late summer	65º - 75º	14 - 21	½" deep, 1" apart	2' after 1st yr.
Beans, Pole	No	—	Early summer through midsummer	70º - 80º	7 - 14	1" deep, 3" apart	Hills-3'
Beans, Bush	No	—	Early summer through midsummer	70º - 80º	7 - 14	1" deep, 3" apart	6"
Beans, Bush Lima	No	—	Early summer	70º - 80º	14 - 21	1" deep, 6-8" apart	12"
Beets & Swiss Chard	No	—	Early summer through late summer	65º - 75º	14 - 21	¼" deep, 1" apart	Beets-3" Sw.Chd-18"
Broccoli & Brussels Sprouts	For spring crop	6 to 8	Late summer for fall crop	65º - 75º	7 - 14	¼" deep, ¼-½" apart	1½' 3'
Cabbage & Cauliflower	For spring crop	6 to 8	Late summer for fall crop	65º - 75º	7 - 14	¼" deep, 1" apart	Cab.-2' Caul. 2½-3'
Carrots	No	—	Late spring through late summer	65º - 75º	14 - 21	¼" deep, 1" apart	1½-2"
Celery	For spring crop	12 to 16	Late summer for fall crop	60º - 70º	14 - 21	1/8" deep, 1" apart	6"
Collards	No	—	Early spring where summers are cool late summer elsewhere	65º - 75º	7 - 14	½" deep, 2" apart	3' apart
Corn, Sweet	No	—	Early summer through midsummer	65º - 75º	7 - 14	½" deep, 3" apart	Hills-3' Rows-12"
Cucumbers	Only short summers	4 to 6	Early summer through midsummer	70º - 80º	7 - 14	1" deep, 4" apart	Groups — 4'
Eggplant	Necessary	8 to 12	—	70º - 80º	14 - 21	¼" deep, ½" apart	3'
Endive	Optional	6 to 8	Late summer for fall harvest	65º - 75º	14 - 21	¼" deep, 1" apart	8-12"
Lettuce	Optional	8 to 10	Anytime except midsummer	55º - 65º	14 - 21	½" deep, ½" apart	Hd.Rm.12" Lf.&Bthd.8"
Melons: Cantaloupes & Watermelons	Optional	4 to 6	Early summer — after danger of frost	70º - 80º	14 - 21	1" deep, 4" apart	Grps.60" Grps.8-10'
Mustard Greens	No	—	Anytime except midsummer	60º -75 º	7 - 14	½" deep, 5-6" apart	12"
Okra	Optional	4 to 6	Early summer	70º - 80º	14 - 21	1" deep, 12" apart	12-18"
Onions	Optional	6 to 8	Bermuda & Green—late summer Other—early spg. thru midsum.	60º - 75º	14 - 21	¼" deep, ½" apart	4"
Parsley	Optional	8 to 10	Late spring through late summer	65º - 75º	21 - 28	¼" deep, ½" apart	6"
Parsnips	No	—	Early spring through midsummer	60º - 75º	14 - 21	¼" deep, 1" apart	4-6"
Peas	No	—	Very early spring and where winters are mild, late summer	60º - 70º	14 - 21	1-2" deep, 2" apart	Rows-2"
Peppers	Optional	10 to 12	Early summer for fall crop	70º - 80º	14 - 21	¼" deep, 1" apart	12-18"
Pumpkins	No	—	Early summer	70º - 80º	7 - 14	1" deep, 4" apart	Grps.6-8'
Radishes	No	—	Anytime except midsummer	65º - 75º	7 - 14	½" deep, ½" apart	2"
Spinach	No	—	Very early spring or late summer	60º - 70º	14 - 21	½" deep, ½" apart	4"
Spinach, New Zealand	No	—	Late spring through midsummer	65º - 75º	7 - 14	½" deep, ½" apart	4"
Squash, Summer	No	—	Early summer through midsummer	70º - 80º	7 - 14	1" deep, 3" apart	Groups-60"
Squash, Winter	No	—	Early summer	70º - 80º	7 - 14	1" deep, 4" apart	Groups 4-6'
Tomatoes	Optional	8 to 12	Early summer for fall crop	65º - 75º	14 - 21	¼" deep, 1" apart	3'
Turnips	No	—	Early spring and late summer	60º - 75º	7 - 14	½" deep ½" apart	6"

A VEGETABLE GARDEN

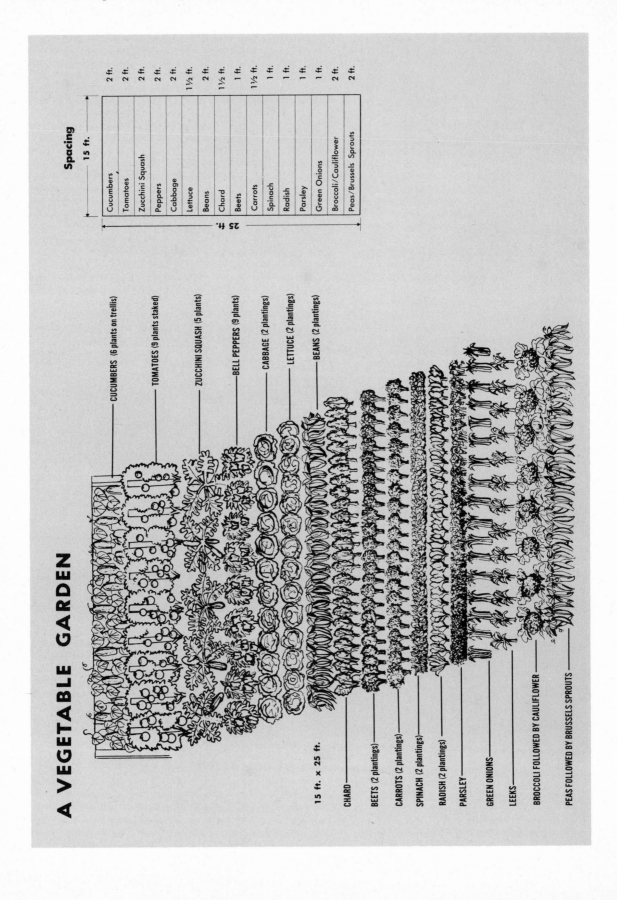

Spacing

15 ft.

Cucumbers	2 ft.
Tomatoes	2 ft.
Zucchini Squash	2 ft.
Peppers	2 ft.
Cabbage	2 ft.
Lettuce	1½ ft.
Beans	2 ft.
Chard	1½ ft.
Beets	1 ft.
Carrots	1½ ft.
Spinach	1 ft.
Radish	1 ft.
Parsley	1 ft.
Green Onions	1 ft.
Broccoli/Cauliflower	2 ft.
Peas/Brussels Sprouts	2 ft.

25 ft.

15 ft. x 25 ft.

CUCUMBERS (6 plants on trellis)

TOMATOES (9 plants staked)

ZUCCHINI SQUASH (5 plants)

BELL PEPPERS (9 plants)

CABBAGE (2 plantings)

LETTUCE (2 plantings)

BEANS (2 plantings)

CHARD

BEETS (2 plantings)

CARROTS (2 plantings)

SPINACH (2 plantings)

RADISH (2 plantings)

PARSLEY

GREEN ONIONS

LEEKS

BROCCOLI FOLLOWED BY CAULIFLOWER

PEAS FOLLOWED BY BRUSSELS SPROUTS